The Century
for Young People

For a complete overview of the most eventful
hundred years in human history, you'll want to read these
companion volumes:

The Century for Young People:
Defining America: 1936–1961

The Century for Young People:
Changing America: 1961–1999

PETER JENNINGS
TODD BREWSTER

Adapted by Jennifer Armstrong

TheCentury
for Young People

Becoming Modern America
1901–1936

DELACORTE PRESS

Text copyright © 1999 by ABC, Inc.
New introduction copyright © 2009 by Brewster, Inc.

This is the first volume of a three-volume adaptation of *The Century for
Young People,* by Peter Jennings and Todd Brewster. Based upon the work
The Century, by Peter Jennings and Todd Brewster, published by Doubleday
Books, a division of Random House, Inc., New York, in 1998.

Visit us on the Web! www.randomhouse.com/teens

Educators and librarians, for a variety of teaching tools, visit us at
www.randomhouse.com/teachers

Library of Congress Cataloging-in-Publication Data
Armstrong, Jennifer.
The century for young people / Peter Jennings, Todd Brewster ; adapted
by Jennifer Armstrong. — 1st trade pbk. ed.
p. cm.
Includes index.
ISBN 978-0-385-73767-8 (v. 1 : trade pbk.) — ISBN 978-0-385-90680-7
(v. 1 : glb) — ISBN 978-0-375-89395-7 (e-book) 1. History, Modern—20th
century—Juvenile literature. 2. History, Modern—20th century—Pictorial
works. I. Jennings, Peter, 1938–2005. Century. II. Brewster, Todd. Century.
III. Title.
D422.A76 2009
909.82—dc22
2009008437

The text of this book is set in 12-point Sabon.
Printed in the United States of America
10 9 8 7 6 5 4 3 2 1
First Trade Paperback Edition

For our children:
Elizabeth, Christopher, and Jack

CONTENTS

INTRODUCTION

If you are one of those people who consider history to be the study of dry and boring facts, please think again. You are in for a surprise when you read these books. Well-told history is as compelling as any great novel or movie. It is full of drama, tension, interesting characters, and fantastic events. That is what you will find here, in this, the history—or should we simply say "story"?—of the twentieth century.

One hundred years may seem like a long time ago, but actually, this is fairly recent history. It is really not too far removed from your life today— and the story of the twentieth century is not just any old story. It is the story of your parents and grandparents, of the world they were born into and the one they helped create. And while some of the events described here happened in faraway places decades ago, you will probably recognize that some things are the way they are now because of what happened then. In other words, this is not only your parents' and grandparents' story; it is your story, too.

One of the most important reasons to study history is to help us understand the present. Think of how old you are today. Now think about your parent or grandparent or even great-grandparent at your age. Without so much as blinking, you can list five things that did not exist in their lifetime. At the beginning of the twentieth century, there was no automobile, no television, no radio, and certainly no Internet. African Americans in the South lived in segregated communities; few women worked outside the home, and none had the right to vote. So how did we get here from there?

Consider global affairs. When your parents and grandparents were growing up, America's biggest enemy was the Soviet Union, which included modern-day Russia and neighboring countries. From the end of World War II in 1945 until 1991, when the Soviet Union collapsed under its own weight, America and the Soviet Union often stood nose to nose. In what we now refer to as the Cold War, a nuclear confrontation between the two countries was a persistent threat, though thankfully, one that was never realized.

Today, the Soviet Union is long gone, replaced, in one sense, by America's twenty-first-century enemy: radical factions of the religion of Islam. Yet you will be interested to read about the events of 1979, when rebels inspired by the Ayatollah Ruhollah Khomeini, the long-exiled spiritual leader of Iranian Shiite

Muslims, challenged what he called the decadent West by overthrowing the American-backed Shah of Iran and installing an anti-American regime. Looking back, we can now say that when Khomeini's followers seized the American embassy in Tehran and held 52 people hostage for 444 days, they gave us a hint of what was to come twenty-some years later: the events of September 11, 2001, the wars in Iraq and Afghanistan, and the threat of Islamic terrorism that you live with today. If you were a small child on September 11, 2001 (or not yet born), that date may seem like just another landmark in our history. But for many others, it is the defining moment of the twenty-first century, *their* twenty-first century. These books will help you understand this and other world-shattering events that shaped our lives.

Another way to think of history is to say that it is the study of change. Consider this: the adolescents of the early 1900s were not referred to as teenagers—the word wasn't even used until 1941—and as late as 1920, children were unlikely to finish, and often even to start, high school. Teens were needed to work the farms in what was still largely an agricultural society. Certainly no one would have imagined that there could be such a thing as a distinct teen culture. The rise of popular music, which came with the phonograph and then the radio, made such a culture possible. So did urbanization, industrialization, and prosperity, which by the 1950s gave families the luxury to let young people stay in school longer, maybe even go to college, and to be "teenagers."

Technology has always been among the biggest agents of change, and as the story of the twentieth century shows, it can introduce itself unexpectedly. When Henry Ford built the first affordable cars in the United States, he imagined that he was creating a machine that would enhance rural life. The first Model Ts had the potential to double as farm tractors. But in the end the automobile had the opposite effect: once people could get into their Fords and travel, they could see worlds that had long been beyond them, and so a kind of new mobility entered American life, with children growing up and moving far away to pursue lives wholly different from those of their parents. Similarly, the first computers—room-sized behemoths created in the late 1940s—were designed almost exclusively as tools for the scientific community, not as the research, communication, and entertainment platforms we consider them today. It was not until the early 1980s that most people had computers in their offices and homes.

The technological, intellectual, and commercial explosions that greeted the twentieth century made many people dream of a day when a permanent harmony would descend over the globe, but sadly, that was not to be. In fact, if there was one common teenage experience the world over, it was that most ancient of human activities, war. Beginning in 1914, large armies in Europe engaged in horrific battle. People called that first global conflict the Great War, thinking that it would be the last such battle in human history. Now we call it World War I, followed as it was by World War II, just twenty years later, and by the persistent late-twentieth-century (and now early-twenty-first-century) fears that we were (or are) on the brink of World War III.

More than nine million people, much of Europe's youth, died in the Great War alone. But as you contemplate such numbing numbers, it may be more powerful to think not just about how many lives were lost, but also about whose lives were lost. If there had been no war in 1914, maybe one of those who died would have grown up to be a scientist who discovered a cure for cancer or a humanitarian who solved the world's hunger problem. Maybe Germans, absent the humiliation of defeat, would never have listened to the perverse racist message of Adolf Hitler, who led that country into the nightmare that could be stopped only by an even greater war that killed even more people. Many historians are now convinced that had there been no World War I, there would likely have been no World War II and no Cold War, for each, it seems, led inevitably to the next.

With all its wars and devastation, the twentieth century may seem like a bleak episode, a sad study. But as you begin your journey through these three volumes, hold that thought. Loud and sensational events always mask slower, deeper trends, and in the twentieth century the more gradual and less sensational changes mark a time of glorious achievement.

Because the forces of liberty did win that protracted battle between East and West, there are more people living in free and democratic societies today than at any time in human history. In our own country, freedom was extended to millions who had long been denied it by persistent traditions of racial, gender, and ethnic discrimination. Only after defeating Hitler were the American armed forces, in 1948, desegregated.

Science produced new weapons of frightening magnitude in the twentieth century, but it also found ways to erase disease and prolong life. Perhaps the century's most significant change is represented by this fact: if you had been born in 1905, you could expect to live only forty-nine years. By contrast, babies born in America today, as you read this, will likely live to seventy-eight, and some—many, in fact—will live to see the twenty-second century.

In a century when it sometimes seemed that some life-changing innovation was being introduced every week, there were also many remarkable acts of human will by people who, stuck in situations that seemed utterly hopeless, found the courage to ask "why?" The twentieth century produced so many more heroes than villains, people like Thomas Edison and Bill Gates, Jackie Robinson and Rosa Parks, George Marshall and Martin Luther King Jr., and it no doubt produced many more who never became famous, who moved quietly, even silently, behind the drama to make life better. They pushed for justice and beauty and good and not only asked "why?" but, thinking of how things could be made better, also asked "why not?" I hope all of you reading this book will emerge inspired by their example. As my colleague Peter Jennings used to write when signing the original edition of *The Century for Young People,* "The next century is yours." To that, I would add a challenge: "Make your mark on it."

—Todd Brewster

CHAPTER 1

Seeds of Change

1901–1914

For generations, people have looked forward to a new century with both hope and nervousness: What will the new age bring? Faced with a mysterious future, they feel both the thrill of possibility and the fear of the unknown. The end of the 1800s carried even more tension than usual because it witnessed the end of many ideas that had ruled people's lives for a long time. Charles Darwin's theories of evolution and natural selection had challenged religion, shaking up people's understanding of their own origins. At the same time, the political ideas of socialism and democracy began to dominate a world that had long been ruled by kings and queens. While vastly different political ideas, both socialism and democracy argued that power should be taken from the elite few and given to the masses. Finally, the growth of science and industry began to change the way people related to the natural environment. More and more, people were leaving the farm to live in a machine-made world, the world of cities. They knew that the city was where the new century would take shape.

In America, these advances in technology promised a bright future. It was American inventors who thrilled the world with new machines, American factory owners who made these new machines for the world's use. Design by design, object by object, they promised to establish a new way of life—not just for a few privileged people, but for all humanity.

Mabel Griep was born in 1896 in Dayton, Ohio, just a few doors down from the Wright Brothers' bicycle shop. She witnessed a landmark event in the history of technology in 1904.

When I was growing up, we didn't have electricity. We used a lot of candles for light, and of course we had gas fixtures. And then outside in the streets, we had street lamps. Every evening at sundown the lamp boys would light the lamps one by one. All the little kids would rejoice when the lamp boys would come, because it meant we could still play outside, even though it was dark.

My father, who was an architect with an office in downtown Dayton, Ohio, was designing and building a new house for us in the country, and it was to be fully equipped with electricity, which was pretty modern back then. There was just so much change going on those early years of the century. I remember when we got our first telephone. You would have to stand at the wall and talk into this contraption, and we shared the line with four or five different neighbors who would all come on the line at the same time. Sometimes you didn't know who was talking to who. Still, it was all very exciting. Life was changing so much and so quickly that it made some people anxious. But not my father; he was extremely interested and excited by what was going on.

One day he came home from work early and said, "Get your things ready. Our boys are going to try a flight today!" My father always referred to the Wright brothers as "our boys." He said, "We'll go out, and if it's successful, we'll be there to see it. It'll make history." Then he hitched our horse, Old Nip, up to the surrey and we headed out to Huffman Prairie, where the flight was to take place. We were good friends with the Wright family. Their bicycle shop was down the street from our home. And when they started working on their flying machine, the word spread pretty quickly around town. Some of the neighbors were pretty skeptical about what they were trying to do. They were always saying, "They're back in that bicycle shop again. I don't know what they think they're going to do. They'll never make a machine that can fly." The Wright brothers were so sold on building a flying machine that none of the negative talk bothered them at all. They just kept working.

Our father had driven us out to Huffman Prairie a number of times. That's the place that Orville and Wilbur used as a testing ground. All the other times we were out there, there was no flying going on. They would just be testing their machine: working on the propeller, or motorizing something, or making it move here or there. But this time my father had heard that they were actually going to make it fly. Now, the Wright brothers had already had a successful flight down in Kitty Hawk, North Carolina, but none of the newspapers really reported on it, and most people didn't believe it actually happened. So as far as we were concerned, they were attempting the impossible that day.

Dad knew of a place at Huffman Prairie that was on an incline, and it offered us a pretty good view of what was going on.

There was much activity going on down in that field, and we had the bird's-eye view of it. Dad was so excited, he turned to us, shaking his fist, and said, "Are you all paying attention to this? Now listen to me, you're going to remember this to your last day." Every time either Orville or Wilbur did something the crowd would inch a little closer to try and see what was going on.

When that plane took off the ground, I just can't describe how I felt. I think I held my breath the entire time, and I'm sure an awful lot of people said a prayer. It was spectacular—just unbelievable. That's all I can say. The plane lifted sort of level at first and then started to rise up. I don't know just how far they went. The whole flight couldn't have lasted longer than a minute, but it proved that it could be done. When the plane landed, the whole field just exploded with applause. And then it got strangely quiet. Nobody could believe what they had just seen. People stood around kind of dumbstruck. Not many people were even talking about it. I couldn't help but think about all of those mouthy people who said it would never happen. I was just exhausted when it was all over. It was like witnessing a miracle.

On an almost daily basis, it seemed, Americans were witnessing miracles of new technology. They were eagerly making way for the future even as they asked themselves these difficult questions: How could this new machine age be made to reflect American values and character? Just what would it mean to *be* American in the frightening and thrilling future that was about to unfold?

If the future had a shape at the start of the 1900s, it was the skyscraper. The architectural wonder of the new era had risen from the ashes of Chicago, which had burned in 1871. When that city was rebuilt, it was not with wood, but with steel, glass, and reinforced concrete. These modern materials were used to create buildings that rose higher than ever toward the clouds. Since exploration and settlement of the western frontier had been completed, it was time to start building upward, into the air itself.

New York built skyward as did few other cities. And as the main port of entry into the United States, it made its skyscrapers a picture of upward mobility to the millions of immigrants who now began pushing toward America. From 1890 to 1910 nearly thirteen million immigrants came to the United States. They came from many countries, all in search of the land of opportunity. Their vastly different backgrounds, their diverse religious beliefs and customs, would pose a challenge to the very idea of what it meant to be an American.

Alfred Levitt, born in 1894, emigrated with his family to New York City in 1911. He described what the experience of coming to America was like.

I was born in a small Russian town of about ten thousand people. We were a poor family. My father made the horse-drawn carriages that the bourgeoisie used on Sundays to promenade down the street. It would take him about six months to build each carriage because he couldn't afford any tools and he had to build each one with his own ten fingers. During the six months it took my father to finish a carriage, the family starved. We had no money, and the rich people wouldn't pay my father until he finished his carriage. It was a very hard life.

My family was part of a population of about two thousand Jews in our city. People yelled out "bad Jew" and "Christ-killer," and they said that we shouldn't be allowed to live. There was a pogrom [a massacre] in 1905 where the Russians looted every store that was either owned or operated by a Jew. I remember my mother pulling me into a hiding place for fear that I would be hurt. It was this abuse against the Jews that made my two brothers decide to go to the United States. In Russia, everyone thought that America was such a rich country that you could literally find gold in the streets. At home there were no jobs for Jews, but in America surely my brothers would find work. They went to New York, worked hard as house painters, and accumulated enough money to buy passage for the rest of the family.

I had never seen an ocean before we got on the boat for America. I looked out onto the sea and saw these huge waves crashing up against the rocks. It was a frightening experience. But then I saw the openness of the ocean, and that great body of water opened my mind to a world that I never knew existed. As we approached New York Harbor I saw the Statue of Liberty, and I was overwhelmed with a feeling of hope for a beautiful life in a new nation. Then we headed toward Ellis Island and I could see the big buildings of New York. It was an amazing sight. The city I came from only had little shacks made of wood and stone. Here everything was big and new. At Ellis Island they looked in my eyes to see if I was healthy and they checked my hair for lice. When they determined that my family and I were not sick, they put us on another boat and we were finally admitted to the United States.

At first I was afraid to go in the subway. I didn't want to climb down into that dark hole. In Russia the only means of transportation that I knew about were horses and bicycles. When I did go in, I discovered a whole new world. There were advertisements that told me what to buy. And I saw people—blacks, yellows, all sorts of different facial looks and ethnic groups, people like I had never seen before. Most of all, I was amazed that I could go anywhere for five cents. I was able to go all the way down to Battery Park, and then, if I chose, I could transfer and turn around and go all the way up to Yonkers for the same nickel.

My first school was on 103rd Street near Third Avenue, but when I discovered that there were too many foreign boys in the same class, I left it, because I wasn't learning the American language fast enough. I wanted to learn the American language because I wanted to understand the American people, the American mind, and the American culture. I wanted to be completely American, and that couldn't happen in a school full of foreign boys. Mostly I wanted to get a good job somewhere, and I knew if I didn't speak English, I couldn't get a good job. So I walked down to another high school in Harlem on 116th Street and asked the supervisor to give me an audience. I told him I wanted to learn the American language and

I wasn't getting it on 103rd Street. He said, "I will give you two questions. If you pass them, you are admitted." He asked me to spell *accident* for him, and I did right away, with two *c*'s. Then he asked me what two-thirds of fifteen was, and I said, "Ten," so he admitted me to high school. In Russia, only a small percentage of Jewish children could go to school, and then it had to be a special Jewish school. In America, I could go to school with everyone else.

For Americans whose ancestors had arrived in earlier centuries, these new immigrants and the new age showed up together—and both required some adjustments. Many Americans were meeting the problems of big-city life for the first time, seeing the grime, disease, overcrowding, and crime that came with rapid growth. Many of them saw these ills as the fault of the foreigners who pressed into the cities. The character of the city was changing so rapidly that some Americans complained that the new immigrants were carrying all the flaws and failures of the Old World to American shores. Called "nativists" for their insistence that people native born in America were inherently superior to those arriving now, these people feared that much was at stake in the new era. If the nation was reshaping itself in the machine age, they wanted to guarantee that the new nation looked like the old one: white, English-speaking, and Christian.

After all, in 1900 America had been a largely homogeneous farm society of only seventy-six million citizens, a nation of dirt roads and horse-drawn carriages, of kerosene lamps and outhouses. And it was a place where many people felt confident of two things: that America was heaven on earth, and that Americans were God's chosen people. The new age, with its teeming cities and smoky factories, challenged such certainties.

Charles Rohleder, born in 1905, described some of the conditions that shaped his childhood in Pittsburgh, Pennsylvania.

When I was growing up at the beginning of the century, times were very hard for the poor. Very tough. There was no welfare to help you out. If you were hungry, the only places you could go to were the missions.

My mother rolled tobacco into cigars at home to try and raise a little extra money. Actually, we all pitched in and helped—my father, my grandfather, me—everybody who was in the house. Back then, very few cigars were actually made in a factory; most were made in people's homes. We would spread out these big leaves of tobacco on the kitchen table and just roll and roll and talk and talk. And then my mother would take them in and sell them to a cigar company, which paid her according to how many she rolled. Of course, she didn't get very much money for them. Cigars at the store only cost about three or four for a dime, so you can imagine what the cigar company paid my mother for them. One time when I was a little boy I got into a box of tobacco clippings and just started chewing. I had seen all of these other people chewing on tobacco, and I thought, "Oh, boy, I'd like to try that!" I couldn't even go to school that afternoon. I was sicker than two dogs.

At that time there were a lot of foreigners moving to Pittsburgh—a lot of immigrants. There were also a lot of blacks moving up from the South. People came from all over because they could get a job right away. People used to say that if you couldn't get a job anywhere else, you could get one in Pittsburgh. There was a Greek family next door to us, and we used to make fun of them because they were immigrants and they spoke a language that we didn't understand. And even though they were really hard workers and were making a go of it, we used to look down on them. I guess it was just ignorance on our part. But back then we just thought that all immigrants were no better than the dirt under our feet. Despite what we thought about them, they worked very hard to try and get ahead—twelve-hour days, six days a week.

As far as the immigrants were concerned, I didn't want to have anything to do with them. I just didn't concern myself with them. I was too busy trying to make a living to fuss with them. I started working when I was six years old, selling newspapers out on the streets.

Pittsburgh was very dirty back then. Everyone burned coal for heat, and it was soft coal, which emits a lot of sulfur and black fumes. Some days you couldn't see the sun at noontime because of the thick smoke from the factories. There were steamboats on the river, and they had these big smoke-stacks. When the boats went under low bridges, the smoke would come right up and cover the whole bridge. There were times when I walked across a bridge and went in clean on one side, but by the time I reached the other side, I needed a new shirt.

And the rivers themselves were even worse. They put these big sewers in, so that everybody could have flush toilets. The sewers just dumped right into the river. I used to see just awful stuff coming out of there.

There was a hospital nearby, and if they had an operation and they chopped off a few pieces of that person—cancer or anything else—they just threw it right in the sewer. Before you knew it, it would come out in the river. And of course, there was the sewage from all the toilets. The worst of it was that kids used to fish right where that sewer came out because that's where the catfish were. I tried it a few times, but luckily I never caught anything.

There were also all of these factories and slaughterhouses and steel mills along the river. You could always tell when the canning factory was processing tomatoes or making chili sauce, because the river would run red with tomato skins. And you would see chunks of fat floating down from the slaughterhouses. At night the sky above the river would look like it was on fire from the open hearths at the steel mills. It was lit just like it was daytime. What a beautiful sight that was; it looked as if the whole city had burst into flames.

At a time when immigrants were looked down on with suspicion, and when city life meant rubbing shoulders with all kinds of different people, it was only natural that the continuing separation between white and black people should be examined with fresh eyes. It *was* examined again at the start of the century, but not to the benefit of black America. It is hard to look back and contemplate the nation's level of bigotry at that time. This was an era when popular magazines described blacks as "coons," "darkies," or "pickaninnies." This was a time when lynchings of black men were considered entertainment in some places in the South.

For a short time after the Civil War it had looked as though the South might advance toward racial equality. But in the last years of the nineteenth century southern whites' power over blacks was strengthened. As long as blacks had been slaves, they were seen as no great threat to white power, even while living and working in the heart of the white community. But now that African Americans were free, they were seen as a threat to the established white community, to be kept at a distance and under control. In the South, new laws robbed blacks of the right to vote, and a new system of segregation was born: Jim Crow laws.

Jim Crow laws meant separate schools, buses, restaurants, rest rooms, and swimming pools. Oklahoma had separate telephone booths. Others had separate school textbooks. This segregation was made legal by the Supreme Court in a case called *Plessy v. Ferguson*. It declared that the U.S. Constitution allowed public facilities to be "separate but equal."

Marjorie Stewart Joyner, an African American, was born in 1896 and grew up with Jim Crow laws in the South.

Even though my grandparents had been born slaves, I was born long enough after slavery that the slave element didn't really exist in my world, or even in my thinking. The beginning of the century was a time when we dreamed that things were going to get better for blacks: better housing and neighborhoods, better schools, better jobs. As a little girl, my dream was to grow up, get married, and have a big house on a large farm with horses and cattle and people working for me. As a people, we had high hopes. But we also knew that to get there we would need an education.

My father was an itinerant teacher. He traveled from one village to another, and would hold classes for children—or adults, for that matter—that had never been to school but still wanted to learn. He would go from village to village after harvesting time or planting time—the times when children didn't have to be in the fields working—and they would hold classes either in a church or at the village hall or even in a clearing out in the woods. Parents wanted their children to have an education. They wanted them to learn to read, write, and do arithmetic, so that they would have the opportunities to make a good living and have a better life.

We were coming out of a time where people actually belonged to other people. And while we no longer belonged to the white man, the white man was still saying, "I don't want my white child seated beside a black boy or a black girl. I want my child to go to a school where there are whites only." It was that kind of prejudice that separated the races. Of course, black people worked with white people all the time. Black people cooked for white people; black people took care of white children; they took care of the white people's houses. Even so, people at that time thought that there must be a separation of the races in order to get along. In the South, we had Jim Crow laws. There were separate facilities for white, and separate facilities for blacks. Out in public, we were always separated from the white people. When people traveled, I mean when *white* people traveled, they didn't want to sit in the same coach or car with black people. So the black people had to sit in a designated Jim Crow car, which was either up in the front of the train, right in back of where they shoveled coal into the furnace of the engine, and cinders would fly all over you, or in the caboose, the last little car on the end of the train.

George Kimbley was also born in 1896 and re-called some of his experiences growing up as an African American in the Jim Crow South.

One day I was walking down the road outside Frankfort, Kentucky, on my way to a white person's house where I was doing some work, when I saw this dance pavilion over across a field. It looked really nice, and even though I was in a white part of town, I got off the road and cut through this field just to get a better look at this pretty pavilion. But then when I turned around to head back, there was a white man standing there with his rifle pointed right straight at my head. Now, I was scared, but I didn't show it. I just walked right up to him and as I passed him I told him that all I did was stop to look at the pavilion on my way to work. I showed no fear what-soever, and he just let me pass.

I was born at a time when they still did things the old slave-time way. They felt that you had to lynch a black man every so often to keep him in his place. And that was the general idea. When I was very young they lynched a black man right here in Frankfort. He was ac-cused of robbing someone, and they strung him up right out in the open. My dad took me down there to see that dead man. He even lifted me up so I could get a good look at him. When I turned around and looked at my dad, there were tears rolling down his face. And he said to me, "George, when you grow up, I want you to do something about the way these white people are treating us black people." I promised my dad that I would, and I'm still trying to do something about it.

Segregation posed a crucial question for black Americans: What path to black progress should they follow? Two influential black leaders offered two differing opinions. W.E.B. Du Bois was the voice of protest. He wanted blacks to push for greater freedom, and for laws that would guarantee equality for black citizens. Booker T. Washington wanted black Americans to improve their own lives apart from mainstream white society, more gradually advancing toward equality. In the end, Du Bois's philosophy won the day and led to the great civil rights movement later in the century.

Everyone, it seemed, was looking for greater opportunity as the century got under way. Now women began to demand an equal share of opportunity, too. Progressive thinkers were split on the issue of women's rights. On one side were the suffragists, who insisted that nothing could be improved unless women had the right to vote. These activists demanded the vote as one of the foundations of democracy. Some suffragists even made their case for the vote by joining a racist argument: If white women were given the right to vote, white votes would instantly double.

Other progressives saw votes for women as *harmful* for women. They feared that if women were given the right to vote, it would suggest that men and women should be treated equally under all aspects of the law. That would make it harder to push for special laws to protect women and children in the workplaces of the new industrial cities.

Suffragists were also attacked by both women and men who were afraid that the vote would destroy families, or at least the traditional division of family responsibilities, with women keeping house and men earning the paycheck. What sort of next generation would evolve, they asked, if all women considered their first duty to be to themselves?

By the early 1910s suffragists had decided to put all their energy into changing the U.S. Constitution to give women the vote. They carried out acts of civil disobedience in an attempt to force the nation's leaders to give in.

Lucy Haessler, born in 1904, grew up in a family of political activists. She first marched for the right to vote when she was ten years old.

I came from a long line of New Englanders. One of my ancestors was on the *May-*

flower, and others fought in the Revolutionary War. My more recent ancestors had been abolitionists in the Civil War. So I grew up with this tradition of public interest and public service. When I was still a young girl, my family moved to Washington, D.C. For me, Washington was an incredibly exciting place. There was the Washington Monument, the Capitol, and the White House. Occasionally my mother would take me out of school to go see Congress in session. We would sit up in the gallery and watch all of these men giving speeches and debating issues. It was very exciting for a little girl.

On Sunday afternoons my parents would invite their friends to our house. These were people who worked for Congress or who worked in government offices, or sometimes they were just enlightened people who were interested in the progressive issues of the day. This was where I first heard talk about women's suffrage—about women's rights and about women getting the vote. It wasn't just that women didn't have the right to vote; they didn't really have the right to own property, they didn't have the right to custody of their children, there were just all kinds of ways in which they didn't have rights. Even at my school, girls weren't noticed as much as boys were. If a teacher asked a question, and the hands went up, it was always a boy that was called on to answer.

I hardly ever heard the suffrage issue discussed outside my home. In school I think only a few of my girlfriends even knew what the word meant, and even they knew very little about the issue. It was at home that I really learned about suffrage. You see, my mother was very involved in the issue. And being the only girl in the family, it was just natural for me to listen to her and to do things with her.

The suffragettes had a big headquarters in downtown Washington. My mother would take me up there on Saturdays when she volunteered to help out with mailings. The backbone of the suffrage movement was composed of well-to-do, middle-class women, both Republicans and Democrats. There weren't many working-class women in the movement. Most of them were too busy working to get involved.

The suffragettes organized pickets and marches and rallies. I was only ten years old the first time I went to a march with my mother. She told me, "Oh, you're too young, you can't go." But I said, "I *am* going, because you're going to win the right to vote and I'm going to vote when I'm grown-up." So she let me march. It wasn't a particularly large parade. We had permission for a group of about fifty women to march from the Capitol to the White House. Everyone there was much older and bigger than me, and they took longer steps than I did. So I had to really hustle to keep up with my mother, but I managed to do it. The more marches that were held, the more you could feel the movement just building and building. In my heart, I knew that this movement was going to go somewhere, and it was going to help with the struggles of women.

What kind of president could lead a country with so many voices crying out for so many things? Theodore Roosevelt became president when an anarchist shot President William McKinley in 1901. Roosevelt, the vice president, was climbing mountains in the Adirondacks of upstate New York when he got the news. At forty-two, Theodore Roosevelt, or TR, as he was affectionately known, was sworn in as the youngest president in the country's history. Physically strong and filled with enthusiasm, he was an enormous inspiration to the nation's young people. In the spirit of the new machine age, TR was sometimes described in technological terms. "A steam engine in trousers" and "a wonderful little machine" were two descriptions of him.

Even though America was busy with its own

growing pains, TR pushed Americans to look outward, beyond the country's borders. He believed that as a great nation the United States had duties toward the rest of the world. Roosevelt felt that Americans were ignorant about foreign policy and were too confident in the protection offered by the oceans on its east and west coasts. He believed that developments in transportation and communication had created a more connected world. Most important, he believed that this new, connected world should be guided by the United States, as if by a father. He flexed America's muscles for all nations to see by parading the U.S. Navy fleet around the world in 1908.

Anne Freeman, born in 1901, recalled what a hero TR was to people at the time.

I feel like I've heard about Teddy Roosevelt practically from the time I was born. My father was such an admirer of the man that it felt as though he was just part of my life. Teddy Roosevelt represented just about everything that my father admired. He had fought valiantly in the war; he had been an assistant secretary of the navy; he was gregarious and forthright. And although he had come from a very rich family, he fought hard for the common man. Teddy Roosevelt had this sense of adventure and spontaneity that my father respected. My father could find no wrong in TR.

I remember him laughing and telling me about how TR was such an independent and headstrong man that people had a hard time keeping track of him, even when he was in the White House. He would get up early in the morning and just take off and leave the White House, unbeknownst to anyone. They didn't have the Secret Service or things like that to keep an eye on him, so he would just take off and go for a walk around Washington before coming back to work. You'd think he would have been a little more careful, seeing as he originally got into office when President McKinley was shot.

One day when my father was working at the Brooklyn Navy Yard, there was this strange man walking around and looking at things. He must have come in as part of a tour group or something, because they had gates and fences to keep people from just walking in. But here was this short man with thick glasses and a mustache walking around as if he owned the place. And then all of a sudden he pulled out a camera and started taking pictures. Well, this one guard immediately went up to the man and told him that he was not allowed to take pictures in the Navy Yard.

"Oh, I can take a couple of pictures," the man replied. "It's okay. I'm not a spy."

"Oh, no," the guard said, "you are not allowed to do that. And if you do, I'm going to have to take you in."

After a gentlemanly argument, the man agreed not to take any more pictures. Well, what this guard did not know was that the man with the camera was actually Teddy Roosevelt. Somehow he had gotten into the Navy Yard and decided he wanted to take some pictures. Even when the guard approached him, he didn't say, "I'm Teddy Roosevelt." He just acted like he was a normal citizen. I think he was trying to test the guard. It wasn't really that odd that the guard didn't recognize TR. You see, back then, before television, the president wasn't as recognizable as he is today. You might see his picture in the paper, but you just didn't see his face all that often. And you certainly wouldn't expect to see him by himself, with a camera, walking through Brooklyn!

Nobody found out that day that it had been Teddy Roosevelt snooping around. But a little while after the episode, the guard received a letter saying that he had been accepted to the Naval Academy—and he hadn't even applied. I guess Teddy was so impressed by the young man's persistence that he pulled some strings to see to it that he got ahead.

To my father, America was a young country full of promise. And Teddy Roosevelt was a president who typified that. He too was young, and he wanted America to be noticed and to be a leader around the world. Teddy Roosevelt had an incredible strength of will that really appealed to new Americans who were trying to make their way. Once he set his mind upon something, he felt he could accomplish it.

One of the goals TR was determined to accomplish was to unite the Atlantic Ocean with the Pacific: to build a canal across the thin strip of land that connected North America to South America. This dream dated back to the sixteenth century. But as the nineteenth century ended, a canal across Colombia's Isthmus of Panama still seemed to be an unreachable goal. A French engineering company had tried and failed miserably. Malaria and yellow fever had crippled or killed twenty thousand laborers. Equatorial rainstorms were another problem, and workers reported seeing tree trunks black with tarantulas. Nature itself seemed to be against the project. After all, no one had ever attempted such a massive reshaping of the earth, a fifty-mile gash from one ocean to the other.

But no president loved a challenge more than Teddy Roosevelt. TR wanted America—and American technology—to be the first to succeed. America would dig the "Big Ditch." Roosevelt himself bullied the nation of Colombia for the rights to dig the canal at Panama. When the government wouldn't agree, he gave unofficial support to the revolt that led to Panama's independence from Colombia. The new nation of Panama quickly agreed to let TR's engineers get to work.

Like Roosevelt himself, the canal was a bridge between two eras. The idea belonged to the 1800s, but the work itself would have been impossible without the technology of the 1900s. The canal's loudest statement about the modern age was the way in which it would be used. TR believed that his nation's chance for world leadership was tied to a bold presence on the seas. It was America's destiny to use the two oceans to guide the world safely into the new century. Easy movement between the Atlantic and the Pacific through the Panama Canal would be key to that plan. To demonstrate their new naval power with flair, officials planned an elaborate opening-day ceremony for the canal.

But it was not to be. Almost at the precise moment when America's great technological challenge was achieved, events in Europe plunged the world into darkness.

CHAPTER 2

Shell Shock

1914–1919

World War I was the bloodiest conflict the world had yet known. Nearly ten million people died and twenty million more were wounded—many of them maimed for life—on three continents. During its biggest battles, the same pieces of land were traded back and forth a dozen times. It left countless widows and orphans, ruined economies, and robbed the world of a generation of young men. Did a scientist die who might have found a cure for cancer? Did we lose a great poet, a wonderful artist? The answers lie buried in the soil of the battlefields.

World War I completely changed the old political order in Europe. When it began, Europe was controlled by a small circle of men drawn from the upper middle class and the aristocracy. Five empires—the Austro-Hungarian, Russian, German, French, and British—dominated the map, and each one (except for France's) was governed by royalty. From Austria, Emperor Franz Josef ruled an empire of fifty million Czechs, Austrians, Magyars, Slovaks, Croats, Serbs, Turks, Transylvanians, Slovenes, Gypsies, Jews, and Poles. In Germany, Kaiser Wilhelm II had the most powerful army in the world and was building a navy to match it. From England, King George V ruled an empire that stretched across more than a quarter of the globe, and in Russia, Tsar Nicholas II controlled a vast nation. Three of these monarchs were related: King George and Kaiser Wilhelm both were descendants of Queen Victoria, and Tsar Nicholas was a cousin by marriage.

Democracy hardly existed in Europe. Politicians and government officials were almost always members of the privileged classes. They were ignorant of the problems of their own poorer countrymen. Though there had been social reforms, most Europeans still led hard lives, toiling in factories, in mines, and on farms. Unhappy with their situations, they had begun to listen to the people who were calling for socialism and self-government.

On Sunday, June 28, 1914, a young Serb named Gavilo Princip fired two shots that would change Europe forever. Frustrated with the treatment of his people under the Austro-Hungarian Empire, Princip longed for the day when Serbia would be a separate nation. The emperor's son and heir to the throne, Archduke Franz Ferdinand, was visiting Sarajevo that day in June. When the archduke's motorcade passed Princip, the young Serb stepped up to the car and shot Franz Ferdinand and his wife.

This murder triggered a feud between Austria-Hungary and Serbia. Russia came to the aid of the Serbs; Germany supported Austria. Then France gave its backing to Russia, and England rushed to defend Belgium, which Germany had invaded on its way to attack France.

The elite classes saw the assassination in Sarajevo as a chance to compete for a larger say in world affairs. They may also have seen it as an opportunity to distract the working classes from their dissatisfaction at home. There were some feeble attempts at diplomacy, but on August 2, 1914, the Great War began. Europe would never be the same.

Many men saw battle as a test of manly virtue and patriotism. War was exciting. War was an adventure. War was honorable. War was a rite of passage. War was a way to sacrifice for one's country. In short, war was good.

But while these men did not realize it at first, modern technology had changed war forever. For centuries, men had thought of war as a competition won by the side with the most grit and determination. But what good was grit in an age of sophisticated war machinery? Modern weapons had put an end to hand-to-hand combat. Machine guns and heavy artillery made an assault on enemy lines nothing more than a suicide run. All a soldier could do was dig in and wait. The long stalemate had begun.

The trenches of the First World War were like graves for the living. Across Belgium and France there were thousands of miles of them, zigzagging this way and that. There were frontline trenches and support trenches, reserve trenches and communication trenches, all tied together to form huge underground cities.

Inside, soldiers lived like rats. The combination of boredom and sudden danger was overwhelming. The trench conditions were so miserable and so new to warfare that they caused a strange psychological illness called "shell shock." Constantly surrounded by dead bodies, listening for the faintest sound of danger, always on the alert for an attack, shooting at an enemy so far away that he was almost invisible, men just shut down. Some went temporarily blind or deaf, or lost the power of speech. Some suddenly shook uncontrollably, lost their memory, or became paralyzed.

The fighting went on for what seemed forever, each side caught up in the illusion that it could just wait the other out. Week after week, month after month, desperate generals prayed that the next day's raid would bring the knockout punch. It never did. One of the most disastrous battles of the war took place in France in 1916, when British troops attacked German trenches in the valley of the river Somme. More than twenty-two thousand men died on the first day of fighting. By the end of the battle five months later, more than half a million British, French, and German soldiers were dead. Yet the Allies never advanced more than seven miles. In fact, from 1914 to the spring of 1918 the line of the western front moved less than ten miles in either direction.

Edward Francis, who was born in 1896, served as a private in the British army from the start of the war until its end and became accustomed to living in the trenches.

The mood among all of us young men was that we couldn't get to be a soldier quick enough. In Birmingham, where I enlisted, they expected to make one battalion, which would be made up of about a thousand men. But within the first few days of war they had forty-five hundred. We had a wonderful time training. I was in a section of about fourteen men, all from the same area. We were like one big family. And then came the great day when they issued us a rifle—the newest Lee-Enfield rifle. You should have seen some of the lads looking at it, those who had never held a gun in their life. We were so itchy to get to France we couldn't stand it. All we were thinking was, "We must get to France before the war's over."

The men training us had never experienced a war where you're in trenches facing each other, with shells coming at you every minute. So we had no idea what it would be like when we got there. We crossed over to France after we finished our training, and we walked fifteen miles to our base camp. When it was our turn to go up into the trenches, the regiment coming out had been there almost since the start, and they looked at us as if to say, "Heh, you're smiling now, but you won't be later."

We learned all about the trenches and their risks and what we had to do to fight the Germans. And of course the morning came when we had to "go over the top"—which meant you'd leap over the trench and cover three, four, five hundred yards toward the enemy lines. So when the officers blew their whistle, we were to dash out of the trenches and make our way toward the German trenches. And it was then that we looked at each other and wondered if we'd ever get through it. Some were visibly shaking. Some were crying. Some were almost shell-shocked before they started. But of course when the whistle went, we had to scramble over. There was always an officer a few yards behind you with a loaded revolver in his hand. Anyone who was a bit slow to go would receive a shot in the foot just to remind him that he was there.

We would only learn later what happened. If we took the trench we went over to capture, then we'd have time to rest and talk. And one would say to the other, "Where's Bill So-and-so?" And someone else would say, "Oh, he's got it. He's killed." And then you see that friends of yours or people you know are missing—some are wounded, some are killed. And you could be talking to a man in the trench, and while you're talking he accidentally looks over the top of it, and in that few seconds he might get it in the head.

We spent a lot of time walking from one trench to the next, and when the weather changed to rain and mud, well, it's almost impossible to describe what that was like. If you've seen pictures of the surface of the moon, it was something like that, only worse—all dug up and wet through with mud. Impossible to walk. To get two miles would take seven or eight hours. Sometimes you were in water up to your waist, and had to walk in it for a week to get to the firing line. And under those conditions, they couldn't bring food or water up to us—all the people bringing it were shot down or shelled. So we were hungry and thirsty most of the time. When we'd been there about six or eight months, covered in mud, wet through practically all day, absolutely chewed up by lice, we used to say, "And to think we wanted to come to this hole."

In our first month there, we could smell the dead bodies. But after a while we took no notice of it. For a person just arriving there, it would stink. But to us, who were used to it every day, we didn't think a lot of it. The noise was always on. And when you'd been as long in the trenches as I was, you could almost say for sure if a shell was going to drop by you by the sound it made.

Practically everyone had shell shock, but there were two kinds: one for the privates and one for the officers. With an officer, at the slightest trembling of the lips, they would be sent to the hospital for a week, and then to England to recover. But privates would get a dose of medicine and be sent back onto the line. That was the difference. You could easily see when a man had shell shock. He was crying, shaking; his face was absolutely a different color. It was all we could do in the trenches to hold him back. Sometimes we'd even sit on him. Because once he got out of the trenches, he was a dead man. Some couldn't stand it and walked out. And inevitably they got shot for deserting.

In the later years of the war we got used to the dead bodies and treated them as nothing, like pieces of wood. Everything had a use. We'd even put the bodies in the bottom of the trench and stand on them to keep dry. Of course, these bodies were recovered later, but if they were left too long, they became skeletons, because the rats chewed on them. Some of them had food which had been sent by relatives from England, and that was a godsend, because other than that we could not have stood up to the conditions we were forced to fight in.

Almost from the moment the war began in Europe, America started its own debate about it. Many German Americans sided with Kaiser Wilhelm. But supporters of the Allies far outnumbered them, especially after one of the kaiser's submarines sank the British ocean liner *Lusitania* on May 7, 1915, killing more than a thousand people—including 128 Americans.

To the growing number of American socialists, the war in Europe was simply a battle between Germany and Britain to see which country could become the greatest commercial power. Other Americans saw the war as a symptom of Europe's decay. If Europe wants to commit suicide, they asked, why should we help? President Woodrow Wilson declared that America would remain neutral.

In Europe, the enormous casualties created doubts about the war among soldiers and civilians. Men returning from the front wondered why they had been fighting. A willingness to question authority took hold: Just who were these people in control of this horrible war? And why should we fight so that they can stay in power?

Many people began to see more clearly the huge gap between the rich and the poor, the powerful and the powerless, the few and the many. As they did, the enemy in uniform seemed less responsible for their pain than the "enemy" sitting on their own country's throne.

In Russia, soldiers had begun the war with the same enthusiasm as the English and the French, and had the same fantasy of a quick end. But, of course, it *was* a fantasy. Russia's war minister had thought machine guns and other modern weapons were cowardly, and sent his soldiers up against the torrent of enemy artillery. Russia lost four million men in just the first year of fighting. By 1916, with an unprepared Tsar Nicholas himself commanding the army, the troops were losing the will to fight.

Both the war and an unusually harsh winter had forced enormous sacrifices back home in Russia. Short of fuel, factories closed. Breadlines stretched around the block. Amid the chaos, the cries of the nation's downtrodden peasants for their own land now merged with the demands of the rest of the population for peace. Russia was ripe for revolution.

The revolt began on February 23, 1917, when a parade of female textile workers erupted in protest against food shortages in Petrograd (St. Petersburg). The next day two hundred thousand workers went on strike. Soon the entire city was shut down. Trams were overturned, and bakeries were looted. Artillery depots were taken over, and the weapons and ammunition were distributed to the rioters.

Hearing of the revolt, Tsar Nicholas rushed back home from the front, but he was stopped a hundred miles from his capital and forced to give up his throne. The February Revolution had overthrown the powerful monarchy of Russia in only a few short days.

Vladimir Ilyich Ulyanov, better known as Lenin, saw the revolt as an opportunity. Lenin was the leader of the Bolsheviks, a small political party that had been calling for an uprising of industrial workers, and was in exile in Switzerland. News of the revolt brought him back to Petrograd, where he was greeted by a crowd of admirers. Most were surprised at the radical reforms he suggested. But they all cheered when he announced he wanted Russia out of the war. The cheers grew even louder when he declared he was in favor of land for the peasants.

Lenin's message dramatically increased membership in the Bolshevik Party, and more than a million soldiers abandoned their duties and returned home to get their share of land. In October Lenin rose to power in an almost bloodless takeover.

Alexander Bryansky, who was born in 1882, witnessed the Bolshevik Revolution firsthand.

I had been a revolutionary from the time I was a child, because growing up in poverty under the tsar's regime had taught me very early about exploitation. My father worked as a tailor, and I had a very hard childhood—sometimes we were starving. I went to work at a very young age and then educated myself. In 1905 I learned about Lenin, how he wanted to change life so that everyone would be equal, so that there would be no poverty and exploitation. This affected me greatly.

In 1914 I was sent off to fight in World War I. I was awarded the St. George's Cross, and then ended up in the Petrograd Reserve Regiment after some time in the hospital. That's how I happened to be in Petrograd in 1917 when the February Revolution happened. Of course, I wanted to take an active part in it. I joined a crowd of workers moving toward Nevsky Avenue. The Cossacks [peasant soldiers loyal to the tsar] were deployed at Znamenskii Square. There was a police officer in charge of the Cossacks, and he shouted into the crowd, "Move back, or I'll shoot!" A woman ran up to him and got his horse by the bridle. She wanted to take him aside. He shot her dead right away. Then the crowd shouted, "Cossacks! Why do you keep silent? Cossacks, go home!" And all the Cossacks rode away.

Then the demonstration moved on along Nevsky Avenue. People shouted, "Down with the war! Down with autocracy!" Machine guns rattled from the roofs where policemen were stationed, and several people were wounded. The crowd hesitated. Then a student, a small man with both hands amputated, cried out: "Soldiers, come on! Defend the revolution! Take them down!" A bunch of people broke into the building, went up to the roof, and took the machine gunners down. Soon all the policemen disappeared from the streets to avoid being beaten.

After the February Revolution we saw that nothing had really changed. The new leaders were not going to put a stop to the war. At home capitalism remained, and life for the poor did not change. There were rallies when Bolsheviks were beaten up by crowds of thugs. But worst of all, there was no bread! Bakeries and shops were stormed to provide the people with food. The starvation was universal.

One morning in April Lenin's sister said that he would be arriving that day. Because it was the second day of Easter, all soldiers were on leave, and all workers had the day off, so we called them all to a rally at the station. Finally the train was coming. And then we saw Lenin, standing in a third-class car. When he came off the train he gave a small speech, saying, "Long live the social revolution!"

I met him a few days later, and my impression was that he was just an ordinary man. He seemed to me just like one of the comrades. I thought such a man could not be bloodthirsty, and he wasn't; he made sure the October Revolution was bloodless.

When that moment arrived, one hundred sailors crept into the palace through a back door and convinced some of the guards to give up fighting against the Bolsheviks. I was outside the palace waiting, and when the sailors opened the gates, I ran up the carpeted stairway. In the very first room I saw cadets standing with their rifles ready. I shouted, "Put down your weapons or you'll get it!" When they saw a big crowd of soldiers behind me, they dropped their rifles and raised their hands. I said, "No one will shoot you. We will let you go free if you promise not to raise arms against the Soviet power." Then all the soldiers left, and only the government members remained. They were all arrested without any violence and released, even the worst enemies of the people. So in this way, Lenin was able to accomplish a revolution that turned the whole world upside down.

Germany's own desperate shortages forced it to target American merchant ships delivering supplies to the Allies in early 1917. Germany knew that this might draw the United States into the conflict but decided that it was worth the risk. After enduring several months of submarine attacks, the United States declared war on Germany.

Still, it wasn't easy convincing Americans to join up without making the country's goals quite clear. Many Americans wondered why the United States should join in Europe's war. President Wilson himself had resisted getting America involved. But as the conflict deepened, he believed that it threatened all of Western civilization. And in that he discovered a reason to spur Americans on to fight. He began to refer to the war as a fight for democracy, a chance to rescue Europe with *American* ideas.

The United States was poorly prepared for a

major military conflict. The army had a grand total of 208,034 men. The air force was made up of about fifty-five dilapidated airplanes. In spite of this, the very idea of Americans participating in the war was a powerful boost for the Allies. The strong, healthy, confident Yankees arriving in Paris in the middle of 1917 brought fresh hope to the war-weary people of France. The Americans had an enthusiasm that hadn't been seen at the front in years. And they were fighting for ideas that had become important to the average European soldier and his family, too: democracy, self-government, and freedom.

Corneal Davis, born in 1900, answered President Wilson's call to fight for democracy.

When I was in my last year of high school down in Mississippi, I read this great speech coming from Woodrow Wilson, who was president at the time. I was so excited by it that I clipped it out of the newspaper and sat down and remembered it by heart. He said, "It is a fearful thing for me to try to lead a great peaceful people into war. It could be one of the most terrible and disastrous of all wars. Because civilization itself could hang in the balance." But here is the thing I appreciated and got excited over. He then said, "Right is more precious than peace. We will fight for the things that we carry nearest our heart. For a universal dominion of rights, by a concert of free people, that is going to bring peace and happiness to all of this world."

That's what he said: "We will fight for the things that we carry nearest our heart." And I read that stuff and went crazy over it. Don't you think that an African American boy listening to that sort of speech would get excited? Wouldn't you, if you couldn't drink out of the same water fountain that white people drank out of? It excited me, really, that's the truth. Oh, yeah, I said, that's the thing, a universal dominion of rights, where everybody is going to have the same rights. "A concert of free people": If you read that speech, you will find those words in there. And I thought I ought to get in there and help to bring about this universal dominion of rights, this concert of free people, because it sure wasn't free down where I was.

So that was one of the reasons I wanted to go off to war, but I also wanted to make some money so I could go to college. So I went down and joined. But the question being debated at that time was whether or not they should really train black officers for the war. There was quite a controversy about whether or not blacks should really go over there and whether they would be, I guess, accepted by the French. They only had about ten thousand African Americans in the armies back in those days, but the number went up to about fifty thousand by the end of the war.

I went over to France in a convoy of black soldiers, led by a black colonel who was highly educated and had all the military knowledge that we needed. We picked up more ships in New York City, an infantry outfit they called the Buffalo Soldiers. There were also a lot of Creoles out of New Orleans who could speak French.

I think we made a great hit with the French. I guess back home they thought the French were going to object to us, but we rounded up two or three French generals, and they gave us ammunition and everything else they had. There were plenty of American marines who didn't want us to go into certain places in Paris—there was no "universal dominion of rights" so far as the marines were concerned, I can tell you. They used to say the nastiest things about us, telling the French women that we weren't even human. But the French people didn't feel that way. I don't know of anyplace where a black person couldn't go in France; if there was such a place, I didn't know of it.

With Americans fighting the Germans in France, patriotism ran high at home—and so did suspicion. Anyone with a German last name was suspected of being a spy. A wild anti-German mood spread across the country. Schools banned German classes. German words were changed: Sauerkraut was called "Liberty cabbage," dachshunds were called "Liberty pups," and hamburgers became "Liberty steak." The Post Office even refused to mail magazines and newspapers that printed articles against the war.

Leon Despres, who was born in 1908, shared the patriotic mood of the country during the First World War.

When America entered the war I was nine years old and completely caught up in the superpatriotism of the times. It seemed to me that the United States had been patient and neutral for a long time, but that they had to get involved because the Germans were cruelly killing people and sinking our ships with their torpedoes. I felt that our soldiers going over were tremendously brave.

This was a time of great bitterness towards the Germans. There was no feeling that the war was the result of long economic rivalries or anything of that sort. It was purely an evil thing, perpetrated solely by the kaiser. Since part of my family was German, we had been accustomed to speaking German around the house, but once the war began we stopped speaking it. We turned our backs on anything German—literature, music, history. A German name was a great liability during World War I. Families changed their names. There was a boy in my class whose last name was Kirshberger, and his family changed it to Churchill. It seemed downright unpatriotic to keep a German name and very patriotic to change your name. In fact, anyone who was known to talk positively about Germany was thought to be a spy.

I was totally caught up in the righteousness of the war, and I wanted to do my bit. I wrote letters to the soldiers and learned to knit scarves for them, though I never really caught on to it, so I don't think my scarves amounted to anything. I had a victory garden, and that was very exciting, though I don't think I ever grew anything more than radishes. We collected salvage for the Red Cross; I was very conscientious in collecting and tying up newspapers, collecting as much metal as I could. They would give you coupons, which you would paste on a card, and when you filled the card, then you could put the card in your window. It was an exciting time, and everything we did—knitting, gardening, rolling bandages, walking in parades—we felt was part of winning the war.

It was a wonderful time to be a young boy. I remember going to see the war games on the lakefront in Chicago. They had rifles and terribly loud explosions and flashes, and I thought it was glorious. That was my idea of war. You know, it didn't occur to me that people were getting their faces blown off, that they were losing limbs, that they were being wounded forever, that young men were being killed. I was aware that young men died in the war, but to me it was kind of a beautiful sacrifice, sad but very beautiful.

Most Americans wanted to "do their bit" to help in the war effort. For the most part American women helped the war cause on the home front, but many responded to the nation's call for service in Europe.

Laura Smith, who was born in 1893, described her life as a war nurse.

The day that the war was declared, my boyfriend went to enlist, and the line was so long they couldn't receive everyone who showed up. I was just finishing nursing school in 1917, and our whole class enlisted with the Red Cross as soon as we graduated. We were sent down to New York, where we marched in a parade wearing our nurse uniforms. Everyone waved their flags and applauded as we went by; there was so much enthusiasm for the war. I don't think we knew what we were getting ourselves into. I wasn't scared at all. I didn't know enough to be scared.

I got my first dose of the real war when they put me on duty in the amputation ward of a hospital in Paris. I had to help a doctor amputate a young man's leg. It was very difficult to look at. That's when I learned what I was going to be up against. I think they put us there just to prepare us for what we would be doing on the front. And what made me so sad was that the boys in the ward were all so full of fun—happy and joking. I just cried all day. I told myself I was going to forget everything, and deliberately closed my mind to a lot of things that even now I can't remember. I can still recall the sound of a leg being sawed off, though, and that's the one thing I wanted to forget.

They sent us out to our evacuation hospital, which was a group of tents about twenty miles from the front lines. Each tent held twenty cots, and the boys were sent down from the front in ambulances. We cleaned them up, dressed their wounds, and let them sleep, but there wasn't too much we could do for them. They came in so dirty, with fleas and all, that some of them had to be deloused, and they were just glad to be clean and out of those trenches. Sometimes they came in so many at a time that we had them lying on the ground outside our tent because there wasn't room for them.

We tried not to attach ourselves to anyone, but my friend and I became so fond of one of the boys that was injured. He had a hole right in his forehead and he couldn't speak except for one word, which was *glass*. One day one of the nurses sang "Over There" to him, and he sang and sang, every word. For whatever reason, the music triggered something in his brain that allowed him, at that moment, to sing. My friend and I wanted to get him to talk again, so we kept him for two or three days, which was something we'd never done with any of the other patients. But we never got him to talk. He was so young, and he smiled all the time and didn't seem to be in any pain, but it was so sad to think that it was his brain that was affected in that way.

The European conflict had a dramatic effect on American society. American businesses took advantage of the European need for food, raw materials, and weapons, and the increased business activity boosted America into a period of prosperity. At the same time, the flow of immigrants into the United States from Europe had dropped off, cutting back on the availability of cheap industrial labor.

These wartime labor shortages helped open many nontraditional jobs to women. Women worked on the railroads, in metalworking and munitions jobs, and as streetcar conductors. This helped change social attitudes and made people more willing to grant women the right to vote.

But perhaps the most enduring effect of the war on American life occurred in the African American community. In 1910 four out of five African Americans lived in the South, where most were tenant farmers. As America's wartime economy took hold, thousands of these men and women made their way to the big cities in the industrial North, looking for jobs in the steel, auto, and mining industries. Black southerners, urged on by visions of freedom and jobs, hoped they would find the promised land. The population shift was so large that this phenomenon was called the Great Migration.

Milt Hilton, who was born in 1910, was part of the Great Migration. He described his journey from Mississippi to Illinois.

When I was growing up in Vicksburg, Mississippi, the South seemed like a happy place to me. My mother had gone to Chicago, so I lived with my grandmother, who was born a slave. I didn't know what the word *segregation* meant. I knew that black people had to do all the dirty work and weren't allowed to go into certain places. Nobody ever had to explain all of this to me; I just knew it. But by the time I was eight years old I had seen my first lynching. I was on my way home from school, and I saw a black man who'd been hung up on a tree. A bunch of white men were standing around him—they had poured gasoline on him and set him on fire, and now they were shooting at his body. I didn't really understand what was happening.

I knew people were leaving Mississippi and going north. It was no problem for a black woman to leave town, but a black man couldn't go to the railroad station and buy a ticket out of Mississippi because the white people didn't want to lose all of that cheap, unskilled labor. In 1910, the year I was born, my uncle was working at a white barbershop in Vicksburg. His friends who had gone up north would write back and tell him what a wonderful place Chicago was.

My uncle wanted to get up there, so he faked a letter from somebody in Memphis and told his boss that he had an aunt who was dying and wanted to see her nephew. His boss read the letter, took him down to the railroad station, and used my uncle's money to buy him a round-trip ticket. He said, "Now, you go up to Memphis and you come on back here, you hear?" My uncle said, "Yes, sir." But of course when he got to Memphis he sold the other half of that ticket and kept on going to Chicago. My mother joined him after I was born. From 1910 to 1917 my uncle and my mother worked and saved up enough money to rent an apartment and bring the old folks and the children up to Chicago.

I was eight years old when we left, and all it was to me was a wonderful train ride. It was all happiness to me—you know, "I'm going to Chicago to see my momma!" And my grandmother really felt good because she had made great progress from where she had started out, being born a slave and all.

We didn't make the morning train, because by this time my grandmother was a pretty old lady, slow getting around. It poured down rain as we waited for the evening train, and the nice little cap my mother had bought me got all wrinkled up. We boarded the train, and the coach we were allowed to sit in was right next to the coal engine, so the smoke and soot were horrible. My grandmother had made her hard-boiled eggs and fried chicken, and we sat back there brushing the coal soot off the chicken and eating it and enjoying every morsel of it. My mother used to love to tell the story of when they met us at the railroad station in Chicago, because we looked so very bad! Totally disheveled. They threw coats around us and took us home to clean us up so we would look presentable.

With America's entry into the war, a new feeling of hope had taken hold in Europe. The stalemate was ready to break. True to his word, Lenin and his Bolsheviks negotiated an end to the war on the eastern front. But even with the Russians out of the fighting, Germany still struggled. American soldiers were pouring into Europe, and the kaiser had to push for victory or give up. In March 1918 the Germans made their last huge effort, but it was not enough. In July the Allies turned the tide and sent the kaiser's forces into retreat.

The treaty ending the First World War was signed five years to the day after the assassination of

Archduke Franz Ferdinand. But instead of ending the hostilities, it continued them by other means. The Allies used the peace treaty to punish the Germans. They demanded that Germany accept all the blame for the war and pay the Allies back all the money the fighting had cost them. The Germans felt stunned. When they heard the terms of the peace treaty, masses of people protested in the streets. What should have been the end of a terrible story became the start of another, for many believe it was Germany's attempt to regain power and avenge its harsh treatment that sowed the seeds of World War II.

Still, some good came out of the war. It toppled cruel dynasties in Austria-Hungary, Germany, and Russia. In their places newly independent countries such as Poland and Czechoslovakia were formed. And it helped make societies all over Europe more democratic. The days of the ruling aristocracy were over. A new spirit of equality spread throughout Europe. Women were given new rights, and in Britain and the United States these included the right to vote.

The old Europe, the continent of kings and queens, was gone forever. Ready to fill the gap were two systems, democracy and socialism, both of which aimed to take power from the elite and give it to the people. World War I truly had destroyed a world. The challenge to the survivors was to create a better world in its place.

CHAPTER 3

Boom to Bust

1920–1929

The 1920s were the decade when modern society began. Americans were excited by the technological advances that were becoming a part of their lives— the movies, the automobile, and the airplane. But they were also a little frightened, for technology was changing the world faster than it ever had before. For many Americans, it was a time when they felt torn between the simple, traditional life as lived on the farm, for example, and the new, exciting Jazz Age that beckoned from the city.

Europe, too, was changing and restructuring itself after the First World War. But the spirit of this decade belonged to America and its thirst for the new. Businesses advertised new mass-produced products. New mass-audience media, such as radio, reached right into people's homes. Women, who could now vote, were showing a new spirit of independence. And new, cheap cars could carry Americans farther from home than ever before.

For some, especially the white citizens of small-town America, these developments set off alarm bells. Some hoped for a return to old-fashioned values. But there was no going back. Americans were busting loose, and the inventions of the age were driving them into the future.

Automobiles had been around for a long time. Henry Ford had built his first car in 1893, and his first Model T was completed in 1908. In 1920 there were already eight million horseless carriages rattling around the muddy, rutted roads of the American countryside. Most of those eight million cars were Model Ts, which cost only $300. Now that the automobile was affordable for so many people, and the engine of America's robust twenties economy, it was beginning to reshape everyday life and thought.

The automobile age created a new sense of freedom and individuality. People could decide for themselves when to travel, instead of having to rely on train schedules. It also brought communities closer together, now that motorists could drive from one town to the next in a fraction of the time it had once taken to go by horse or on foot.

Even the countryside began to change to make way for cars. Road building went into high gear. With each new mile of highway, it seemed, something new popped up: the first traffic light in 1922, the first shopping center in 1924, the first national road atlas in 1924, the first motel ("*motor* ho*tel*") in 1925, and the first public parking garage in 1929.

The joy of the automobile was the car itself and the places it could take you. Whether you were going from a small town to a bigger one or from a bigger town to a city, cars were literally the vehicle of escape. Betty Broyles, who was born in 1919, described how the car changed her family's life.

In the days before the car and the radio, we found ways to amuse ourselves. I always loved to read, and that was a very important source of entertainment, particularly in the winter.

Then, when I was quite young, my aunt bought her first car, a two-toned brown Dodge. The salesman gave her the driving lessons. And I got to ride along in the backseat, which was a big thrill for me because I learned as much as she did. I watched all the things he told her to do. And that was how I learned to drive. At that time we didn't have to have a driver's license, so I really did quite a bit of driving by the time I was thirteen. And got along fine.

Then in the summer we were able to get out and really have some good trips. We saw all of the Indiana state parks, for instance, in the first year or two. It was such fun driving.

My aunt liked to stop before it was dark. So by four o'clock or so we'd start watching for a tourist court or a tourist home. Many people would rent rooms in their homes to tourists. And they'd have a sign in the yard advertising tourist rooms, usually about a dollar a night. There were many tourist courts available, too. They featured separate little cabins, and they would rent for maybe two or three dollars a night.

The roads were sometimes surprisingly good. From Warsaw to Fort Wayne we'd drive on Highway 30, which was a cement road. Of course, it was narrower than it is now, and just two lanes. If you had a breakdown—and there were plenty of breakdowns—you'd hope you'd find a gas station soon. But even if you couldn't, there were always plenty of people glad to help you. There was no concern as far as being robbed or mugged. You felt very safe.

In the late twenties my father was stationed at Charleston, South Carolina, in the navy. So we decided that the three of us, my aunt and my grandmother and I, would go down and visit him. That involved, of course, going from Indiana to South Carolina. And we took several days to do it. I can remember driving into the area of the Smoky Mountains, on a gravel road from Gatlinburg into the Smokies. A gravel road! But we made it fine to Charleston.

On that same trip, after we left Charleston, we drove on to New York City. I remember going through the Holland Tunnel. I never had been in such a large tunnel before. And to go under a river, it just seemed incredible. And the lights impressed me so. We had a wonderful time in New York City.

We stayed with a relative who was a housemother for a musical sorority. We went to Central Park, and she took us down to watch the sailing of a ship, the *Europa*. We got to go on board the ship and see all the tourists getting ready to leave for Europe that night. We enjoyed New York, stayed for a few days, and then drove home, stopping at our little tourist courts along the way.

The car was so attractive it even altered how people thought about money. While Ford continued to produce the plain black "Tin Lizzies," the new General Motors company manufactured cars that had style. With hydraulic brakes, chrome plating, and six cylinders, the GM cars were more expensive, but people ached to get their hands on them. So GM offered a new way to buy them: the installment plan.

Installment buying, or buying on credit, was a slightly shameful idea for most middle-class Americans at the time. It was something that only poor people did. But the lure of the new cars and the spirit of excitement that filled the 1920s began to change this attitude. People wanted new cars, and they wanted them *now*. The auto age paved the way for an era of buy now, pay later.

Now that people felt comfortable buying cars on the installment plan, they began buying other things on credit, too. By the end of the 1920s more than 60 percent of all sewing machines, washing machines, vacuum cleaners, refrigerators, and furniture were bought on credit. And one of the most popular items was the newest communications technology: the radio.

Amateurs had been fooling around with makeshift radio sets since the first years of the century. As early as 1911 instructions for building a radio receiver were listed in the Boy Scout manual. Radio had a quality of adventure, especially when it involved listening in on signals from navy stations. During World War I all civilian radio broadcasters were ordered to be silent, to keep the airwaves open for military use. But even when the war was over, most people still thought of radio broadcasting as an oddball hobby.

With the licensing of the first stations in the early twenties, that began to change. Now there was actually something to listen to between the static, even if families still had to build their own receivers. It was a thrill to see how a few wires and tubes could make a voice come out of thin air. A radio, like a car, could take you to faraway places.

In 1922 radio really took off. At the beginning of that year there were 28 stations; by the end of the year there were 570. Albert Sindlinger, who was born in 1907, was like many young boys of the time, tinkering with a homemade radio, trying to catch an echo of the future from out of the air.

When I was about seven years old, in 1913, my uncle gave me a book by Marconi on how to build a wireless [radio]. The Marconi book prompted me to build my first radio, which utilized a Ford motor. At that time, the Model T was the Ford car. And if you took the spark system out of an old Model T, you could build a wireless spark transmitter. I had a cousin about five miles away, and we used to talk to each other by the spark radio.

A few years later I read about the invention of the vacuum tube and discovered someone in Marion, Ohio, who had one that he wanted to sell. I think the price was fifty-three dollars, which was a lot of money. But

I had a newspaper route and had saved up. And so in the summer of 1920 my uncle drove me to Marion. It happened that Warren Harding, the presidential candidate, was passing through Marion that day in a train heading for New York. So I got to meet him and [future president] Herbert Hoover, who was fascinated by my vacuum tube. The next day we drove back home. We had to wait overnight because car [head]lights weren't powerful enough for true darkness then.

About four or five days after I had gotten the vacuum tube hooked up, I started to hear music coming across the wires. Music! And then, between the music, I could hear somebody talking. It took me five or six evenings to put together what was being said, but I finally determined that it was "I am Dr. Conrad. I am experimenting with radio station eight-XK. If anybody can hear me beyond Steubenville, Ohio, to the west please call me long distance." And he gave his telephone number.

Now, there were only three telephones in our system. My father, as school superintendent, had one, the mayor had another, and the minister had the third. But none of us had ever called long distance. So I ran across the street and knocked on the door of our local telephone operator and told her that I wanted to make a call to Pittsburgh, which was about a hundred miles away. It took her about forty-five minutes to go through the manual and figure out how to make the long-distance call. But when we finally got through, I don't know who was more excited, Conrad or me. His signal was getting out a hundred miles! For the next three weeks he would go on the air and I would go on the telephone and tell him whether his signal was better or worse.

Soon I got a letter from him, and he said that on the night of the presidential election of 1920 he was going to broadcast the election returns in what would be the first official radio broadcast, and he wanted me to come celebrate the moment with him at the station. My family went to Pittsburgh with me, and when he met my father, Conrad thought he was the guy he had been speaking to these many months, not some thirteen-year-old kid!

The transmitting station was at the top of a tall building, and I went in and took an elevator to the top. It was my first elevator ride, and I was impressed that there were so many elevators in the building. Then I found out that this was known as the K Building of the Westinghouse Company, where they tested elevators. So it was a building of elevators. And on the top floor they had built this little shack. There were two men in there doing the transmitting. They had two microphones. One was held with rubber bands in front of a Quaker Oats box that had been propped in front of the speaker of a Victrola. This was the mike they used to transmit music. And then the other microphone was used for voice.

Now, by January of 1921 I had decided to build my own broadcast station. I built a hundred-watter and then applied for an experimental broadcast license. In March I got a letter saying, "One of my first official duties as Secretary of Commerce is to award you this license. Aren't you that young fellow I met back on the railroad platform in Marion, Ohio, with that vacuum tube? What's a fourteen-year-old kid going to do with a broadcast station? Signed, Herbert Hoover."

Another new entertainment form was on the rise, one that was pure magic: the movies. By the mid-1920s there were twenty thousand movie theaters across the country, in small towns and big cities alike. Every place that was anyplace had a movie palace, and everybody who was anybody went at least once a week.

Like radio, movies helped create a shared

national culture. Teenagers from Maine to California looked to the movies to see the latest fashions and hear hit songs. Charlie Chaplin was the biggest star, but moviegoers flocked to see screen idols such as Rudolph Valentino, Clara Bow, and Douglas Fairbanks.

Even more than cars or radio, movies let people escape to exotic places. In big cities the theaters were designed to be the fanciest places in town. Because the earliest films were silent, many of these movie palaces had enormous pipe organs, or a full orchestra, to provide the soundtrack. The moment people walked through the doors of these extravagant theaters, with their plush velvet curtains and crystal chandeliers, their imaginations soared.

Pete Pascale, who was born in 1914, grew up in New York City. When he stepped into a movie theater he felt the same thrill people all across the country felt.

When I was a kid in East Harlem, there were a lot of movie palaces with names like the Cosmo, the Beaumont, and the Stadium. And then we had the Liberty Theater, which was smaller and showed the older movies. We used to go to the Liberty because it was easy to sneak into. Sunday was the big day there. A lot of people would come and bring their food with them in a pail. They would sit in the theater, watch the movie, and eat their Sunday afternoon dinner. The place was always a mess. And you had to be careful where you sat because the guys in the balcony eating their dinner would set their pails on the railing and forget about them and then some macaroni would end up falling on your head. We kids would watch it happen and then laugh like hell. It was crazy, but we had a great time.

Back then, many of the studios were in New York, and we could go to them and watch movies being made. We got to see many of our favorite stars—Harold Lloyd, Douglas Fairbanks, Tom Mix. We got to see Harold Lloyd making a movie on 116th Street, hopping onto a bus and hanging out of the window. And then *The Jazz Singer* came out, and it was all anyone could talk about: "Did you see the talking picture?" It was a big topic, this new step in the movie industry, because this was our main means of recreation, just going from one theater to the next, and suddenly after years of watching the silents, we had sound!

The 1920s were energized by yet another magical machine, the airplane. Aviation had grown slowly since the Wright brothers had flown the first crude machine in 1903. By the mid-1920s the airplane seemed more likely to become a thrilling toy than a means of transportation. Carnivals and country fairs featured daredevil fliers. They performed stunts such as wing walking and parachute jumping, and people could buy a ride for $5—if they dared! While the flying machines were exciting, the general feeling was, "You'll never get me up in one of those things." Then came Lindy.

In May 1927 Charles Augustus Lindbergh flew his single-engine *Spirit of St. Louis* from New York to Paris. It was four hundred miles farther than anyone had ever flown before, and he did it solo. Few people thought he could make it. Less than a month before, two French pilots trying the same route had been killed in a crash. But Lindbergh was determined to succeed.

The weather and visibility over the Atlantic Ocean were so poor that sometimes Lindy flew only ten feet above the waves. After seventeen hours he was so exhausted that he slipped into hallucinations. He slapped his face, opened the window for air, and forced himself to stay awake. Twenty-six hours into his flight he saw a bird, and then a fishing boat. "Which way to Ireland?" he called out to the surprised fishermen. At last, thirty-three and a half hours after leaving New York, he landed in Paris. The whole world cheered.

I was seven years old when I took my first ride in an airplane. It was just after World War I. There was a man out on Long Island who sold rides in a plane he had designed. He would sit there in the middle of this potato field with a big sign: Rides for $5 and $10. I was strapped in on my father's lap, while my little brother sat on the pilot's lap. As we went up over Long Island the clouds parted and we looked out over the fields. It was like a fairyland. The streaks of sun came down all around us and changed colors. And from that moment on, I knew I wanted to fly planes.

When people saw that little children like us were willing to go up in the plane, they felt it must be safe after all, and they lined up for rides. We brought in so much business, the pilot began to give us free rides week after week. By the age of twelve I felt that I knew all there was to know about flying, but my father told me I'd have to be eighteen before he'd let me go up alone. I cried on my mother's shoulder and begged until finally, when I was fifteen, she let me take lessons. After two and a half flying hours my instructor told me it was time to do my solo. I was terrified, but I told myself, "You've always wanted to do this, and now you've got to do it." And once I got up there around one thousand feet, it was like I was home. That's the only way I can describe it.

At the age of fifteen I was flying and hanging around with some of the best pilots in the world. We were having so much fun flying around in those primitive planes. And they were primitive! If your engine didn't give out, that was considered a great flying day. We got to be experts at crash landings because you'd be flying along and suddenly have no engine. You'd look down and find an open field and think, "Well, gee, I can probably make it down there," and make a sudden landing.

We had no radar, and no way of communicating with the ground once we took off, because radios were still too heavy. We navigated by using railroads or by just looking for landmarks.

When I was seventeen I pulled my first major stunt—in order to prove myself to the male pilots. There was one who had just lost his license for crashing a plane while trying to fly under the Hell Gate Bridge on the East River. He was hanging around and griping about being grounded while "this little girl" was allowed to fly, and I decided to show him by trying the stunt myself. When I told my family, my father said, "Well, I don't like the idea of you doing it, but if you were to fly under all four East River bridges, they'd certainly never forget that." So I did. Because of my age, it was supposed to be a secret, but a whole gang of newspaper reporters and newsreel photographers showed up. The Brooklyn Bridge turned out to be the only tricky part of the stunt—I had to fly through it sideways to avoid a big destroyer ship coming upstream. This was the shot they showed in theaters all over the country. The Department of Commerce sent me a letter reprimanding me, but enclosed in the envelope was a note from the secretary asking for my autograph!

Everyone thought of us as daredevils. Many people also thought we were all crazy. I still have letters from people who seemed to think we were from outer space or something. But after Charles Lindbergh's flight, we could do no wrong. It's hard to describe the impact Lindbergh had on people. Even the first walk on the moon doesn't come close. After Lindbergh, suddenly everyone wanted to fly, and there weren't enough planes to carry them.

There weren't too many women fliers in the twenties, so I was kind of an oddity. But I was lucky in that no one ever gave me a hard time about it or harassed me. Strangely enough, though, when I would lecture to women's groups there would always be someone saying, "Well, she really belongs at home. A girl her age should be married. What right has she got to be out there wearing pants?"

More and more women were stretching their wings in the 1920s. They ventured beyond their traditional role as housewives, cutting their hair, wearing shorter dresses, and even aspiring to careers of their own. But this new freedom came at a price. By the late 1920s, there was one divorce for every six marriages—up from one in seventeen in 1890. In spite of new opportunities, women's options in the workplace were still limited.

Lillian Hall Gerdau was born in 1913. She described her attempt to move up the corporate ladder.

Since money was scarce in my family, it was very important for me to start working as soon as I could. And I was very fortunate to get a job with a publishing company, which I liked a great deal. After about one week in the business world I was absolutely in love with the corporate structure. But it was hard for women to get ahead, and we weren't encouraged to do very much. After two years with the company I was promoted and became a correspondent in the distribution department. But I was told, "When you correspond, be sure you don't sign your letters 'Lillian Hall.' You must write 'L. M. Hall,' because we do not want the news dealers to know that they are dealing with a woman." This didn't really bother me, because I was so thrilled that they were letting me do it; I was the only woman doing something at that level. Of course there were two men doing my same job, and they were making $35 a week to my $22.50 a week. But after that promotion, I was so excited, I thought, "Oh boy, I can just see myself becoming circulation director here." So I asked my boss what I should do. And he said, "Why, Miss Hall, you can't be a circulation director, you're a woman. The best thing for you to do is to train yourself so that you can be a good secretary." I was terribly disappointed.

Florence Arnold, born in 1918, watched the conflict between her conservative mother and her daring older sister.

My mother was not very contemporary. She was very rigid and so my older sister and I were brought up according to very strict lines of deportment. We were not to flirt with anyone or wear too much makeup. We were to dress modestly, and we were never to be seen anywhere that ladies did not belong, which was just about everywhere. But my sister defied all of that. She was a flapper. She worked at the phone company, and she wore beautiful short dresses, fur coats, coach-style hats that covered up her head like a turban, and—of course—the galoshes, always unbuckled. That's where the term "flapper" came from because these things flapped, flapped, flapped. The day my sister came home with bobbed hair, my mother took one look at her and retired to the couch with her "aromatics"—her smelling salts that kept her from fainting. When my sister decided she wanted her own apartment, you can imagine how my mother reacted. She refused to let her move out until she was married, so my sister lived at home until she was forty-one years old!

The vibrant national culture of the 1920s found its voice in a new kind of music—jazz. Jazz began in New Orleans during the previous century. Then it traveled north with the Great Migration of African Americans and settled in Chicago. There it took on a new sound. Now it had "swing," a danceable sound that pointed to the influence of white musical styles as well. In the 1920s jazz became America's music.

Night after night, jazz lit up cafés and clubs, especially in the New York City neighborhood of Harlem. Many African Americans had moved out of the agricultural South and become city people. From 1920 to 1929 New York City's black community grew six times larger. By the middle of the decade Harlem was almost entirely black, and it was a national center of entertainment featuring the new, truly American sound.

With so much attention focused on black entertainers, African American culture thrived. Harlem poets, playwrights, and essayists produced powerful work dramatizing the African American experience. This "Harlem Renaissance" helped broaden people's understanding and appreciation of black life.

Howard "Stretch" Johnson was born in 1915. He described what jazz and the Harlem Renaissance meant to him.

As a young boy, growing up in Orange, New Jersey, I had the opportunity to meet Willie "The Lion" Smith and J. P.

Johnson, two of the great piano players of the time, who also happened to be friends with my mother. They would commute from Harlem to Orange to record piano rolls at a local music studio. At the end of the day they would get together with my mother and her sisters and cousins, and it would be party time in the community. It was exposure to musicians like these that led me to read about and appreciate what was being called the Harlem Renaissance, where artists, musicians, and writers were beginning to come forward.

The time was ripe for a renaissance back then. After the defeat of the kaiser in Germany, a spirit of optimism and positive expectation swept across Harlem. The Allies won the war for democracy, so now it was time for something to happen in America to change the system of segregation and lynching that was going on. In Europe, the black troops were welcomed as liberators; so when they came back to America, they were determined to create a situation that would approximate the slogans they had been fighting for. They wanted democracy at home in the United States. And this general idea helped feed the concept of the renaissance.

A lot of people wonder how there could

be joy and optimism in a community under the conditions of segregation and discrimination. But the black community had two very important forces that enabled it to survive and grow. One was the church, and the other was the entertainment world, where you had jazz.

The first time I was truly seized by jazz was in 1927, when I heard Duke Ellington broadcast from the Cotton Club. When I heard that music, that sound that Ellington created, it just went through me: *rah . . . rah . . . dah . . . dom . . . bah*. I still love that music today.

Not everyone shared this enthusiasm for the Jazz Age. If there was one attitude that matched the excitement about the new in the 1920s, it was nostalgia for the "good old days." Hadn't America once been a place where your neighbor looked like you, talked like you, thought like you? In the 1920s people who thought like this began to glorify a past that was mostly white, Anglo-Saxon, and Protestant. Many traditionalists looked for comfort by embracing a literal interpretation of the Bible. They called themselves "fundamentalists," and the subject they hated most was evolution. They worked hard to make the teaching of evolution a crime. In Tennessee, they succeeded, leading to a sensational trial in 1925. Called the Monkey Trial, it featured two famous lawyers: William Jennings Bryan, who argued for the state against the teaching of evolution, and Clarence Darrow, who defended John Scopes, the high-school biology teacher who had taught evolution.

People across the country eagerly followed this dramatic fight between the traditionalists and the modernists. In the end Scopes was found guilty of teaching evolution (though he was only fined $100). But it was Clarence Darrow's defense of science and truth that left a more lasting impression on Americans.

Some traditionalists who wanted to restore old-fashioned morality turned to the Ku Klux Klan. In 1921 the Klan had more than a million members spread across the North and South. By 1924 it boasted four million members. Earlier in the century the nativists had spoken out against new immigrants. Now the Klan revived those feelings. It stirred up hatred of Asians in California, Mexicans in Texas, Jews in New York, and Catholics in the Deep South. The Klan appealed to people who believed that their jobs and their very way of life were threatened by "modern" life and the increasing numbers of nonwhite, non-Protestant, and non-Anglo-Saxon immigrants.

Many people cheered the Klan on and put members in powerful positions. By 1924 the Klan had become so powerful that it had members in the governments of at least six states. Future president Harry Truman almost joined the Klan himself. Tempted by the political benefits it would bring him in Missouri, Truman gave $10 to a Klan organizer. Then he was told that if he won the election, he wouldn't be allowed to hire Catholics. Truman took his $10 back.

Carl Leisure, who was born in 1913 on his grand-parents' farm in Indiana, had firsthand experience with the Klan—and so did almost everyone he knew.

A great many people think of the Klan as simply a hate organization, and that it was. Hate is probably the easiest emotion to teach. It's very easy to be "us" against "them," and that, really, was a large part of what the Klan was about. My parents both belonged to the Klan, and so did my sister and I.

But the Klan was also a natural out-growth of the time, and movements like it were all over the world. We were changing from an agrarian society to a manufacturing society, and the Klan was a reaction to it. People in Indiana had always been farming people. The land was there, and that was your life. It was stable and renewable. But suddenly, in the twenties, the farming went sour and we changed over to a manufacturing existence.

Anything that fought against the changing world was welcomed in these quarters, and the Klan was certainly that even if it was trying to preserve a society that was no longer preservable. The Klan taught the sanctity of the home. They wanted prayer in school. They wanted you to follow the Bible as long as you didn't admit that any part of it was Jewish.

Every businessman who was not Jewish belonged to the Klan, not necessarily because they believed in what the Klan said but because it was good business. Most ministers belonged to the Klan. Many teachers belonged to the Klan. In this state, we even had a governor who belonged to the Klan.

The hatred was big. All new immigrants, regardless of where they came from, were bad. If they happened to be from England, that was pretty much acceptable. Some immigrants from Germany were acceptable. But Irish immigrants were more "them" than "us," because they tended to be Catholic and all Catholics, of course, were "them." Jews, of course, tried to control all the wealth. That was what the Klan claimed. Jews were international, and anything international was suspect. And Negroes were unacceptable, of course. Even Chinese were a no-no, but we didn't have very many, so we didn't hate them much. You can only hate what you have. We felt like we were just engulfed in a sea of people who were not us, and had to fight back.

Then it all collapsed. After some scandals, people lost the faith in it. When the power started to dissolve, the whole thing disintegrated. And it was a good riddance.

If there was one issue that united traditionalists with modern reformers in the twenties, it was the Eighteenth Amendment to the Constitution. That amendment prohibited the sale of alcohol, and the period after it became law in 1920 is called Prohibition. Some supporters felt that alcohol was immoral. Others hoped that Prohibition would put a stop to the destructive influence of alcohol on family life. The Klan saw Prohibition as a way of rejecting the wine-drinking immigrants from countries such as Italy and Greece. But Prohibition had unexpected results.

What Prohibition actually did was to encourage crime on a scale never seen before in America. Smuggling alcohol into the country (bootlegging) became a big business. But it wasn't just big-time bootleggers who were breaking the law. Average citizens carried hip flasks, visited "speakeasies," and brewed their own alcohol in stills they bought at the hardware store. Meanwhile, many of the so-called law enforcers were getting rich off bribes. And organized crime, which controlled most of the illegal liquor trade, was booming. Al Capone ruled Chicago, and gangsters controlled other cities, too. Gangland murders filled the newspapers.

By the late 1920s there were thirty-two thousand speakeasies in New York City alone—twice the number of bars before Prohibition. In many places around the country liquor was sold publicly in open defiance of the police. The Eighteenth Amendment had made society less law-abiding, not more moral.

John Morahan, who was born in 1915, helped his family run a typical speakeasy in New York City.

My mother was Irish, from county Sligo, and for her making booze was a family tradition. In Ireland everyone makes their own stuff. So when she got here to New York, she and my father bought some rooming houses, and when Prohibition hit, she just started making booze in the kitchen and selling it from the ground floor. She was a real businesswoman, my mother, and I guess I took after her. As a teenager, I was already driving around in a Nash convertible making deliveries and running four speakeasies.

The way it worked was we'd make some of our own stuff, and the rest we'd bring in from Scotland or Canada. Our speakeasies were just like a regular bar you'd see today except for the door with the peephole in it. We had to be careful who we let in, and we knew our customers on a first-name basis— they were like family. If a stranger were to come in and he turned out to be a government agent and you sold him anything, you'd be finished. The minute you asked him for the money, he'd pull out the badge and pow! They would put a big lock on your door and close your joint down.

We had to watch out for cops, too, but we knew quite a few of them. Some of the best customers we had were cops. Sometimes they'd pay for their drinks, but mostly we'd take care of them, you know, if they were working the beat. When we'd bring in barrels of beer, we'd give the beat cop a dollar a barrel if he was watching. This kind of thing was going on across every level. If the Prohibition agents were going to raid us, we would usually get a call from the police captain at the desk telling us ahead of time. So we'd move everything next door, and they'd come in and look around and there'd be nothing. Everyone was on the take back then, all the way up to the mayor, Jimmy Walker. In fact, we used to make deliveries to his house every week.

We couldn't always know when they were coming, though. Once, when I was about fifteen, the Prohibition agents came and broke down our door with an axe. I grabbed a broom and made like I was sweeping the joint. And when the guys came in they said, "Get the hell out of here. You're too young to be working at a place like this." Meanwhile I was running the joint! So they locked up the bartender and, boy, were they surprised when I was the one who came to bail him out. This kind of thing didn't happen to us too often, though, because we ran a respectable joint. As long as your joint was respectable, you were generally okay.

In spite of nostalgia and the Klan, in spite of Prohibition, the 1920s drove ahead with wild excitement. Radio, movies, airplanes, automobiles, jazz—everything screamed, *Go, go, go! Faster! Louder! Richer!* Americans were buying on credit, living it up, and expecting that their prosperity would go on and on. So when the stock market crashed in October 1929, few people were paying attention, and few people realized that the party was about to end.

CHAPTER 4

Stormy Weather

1929–1936

The stock market crash of 1929 was a catastrophe. But it was just one part of a much bigger picture of pain and suffering in the 1930s. Suddenly the bright lights of the Jazz Age went dark. It was as if America had gone from a carefree summer into a freezing winter.

Only a small percentage of the country was directly affected by the stock market crash in October 1929, when almost $30 billion went down the drain in a matter of days. And many of those involved thought the situation would change for the better quite soon. But by the early months of 1930 it was clear that more than just the stock market was in trouble. Businesses were closing, jobs were scarce, and banks were shutting down, wiping out the life savings of millions of people. The nation, and the whole Western world, sank into what is called the Great Depression.

In 1930 some twenty-six thousand American businesses collapsed. The next year even more went out of business. By 1932 almost thirty-five hundred banks had closed. Twelve million people were out of work (almost 25 percent of the workforce). Still, it is hard to understand what that means without imagining the scenes people saw every day. Lines for free meals at soup kitchens stretched for blocks; fathers knocked on their neighbors' doors to ask for a piece of bread so their children could eat; people fought over garbage cans behind restaurants, looking for scraps of food; families sat on the sidewalks surrounded by their furniture after being thrown out of their homes. America had once been the land of possibility; now it was the land of despair. Americans looked back longingly at the happy-go-lucky twenties, wondering what had gone wrong.

To this day, economists debate the causes of the Great Depression. One common explanation for this disaster is that wages had not kept up with the growth of industry in the twenties. Factories had been churning out more products than ever before. But because the owners of the industries were keeping most of the profits, fewer and fewer people could afford to buy what the factories were making. For a little while the buy-now-pay-later shopping spree had disguised the problem. But eventually people had to pay their bills. When their wallets got emptier, they stopped buying new cars and radios and furniture. In turn, the factories had to slow down production. That meant laying people off from their jobs, which meant that people had even less money to spend.

> Clara Hancox, born in 1918, grew up during the Great Depression, and her experience was shared by millions.

My parents migrated to New York from the Ukraine in 1916, and when I was a young girl we lived in the slums of the Lower East Side. During the 1920s we didn't know there was going to be a depression—we were just building ourselves up and struggling along. We lived in a poor place, but we were never desperate. My father started working in the flooring business, and as the building trade boomed he really started making money. This allowed us to move uptown to the Bronx, which to us was like living out in the country.

My father was doing very well, and he got this marvelous order to do the floors in a building that could be called a skyscraper in those days. He went to the bank and borrowed a huge sum of money to buy the materials. And just as the work was about to begin, the market crashed. We weren't even paying attention to the stock market, so we didn't really know what was happening at the time. But almost overnight it was like a bomb had fallen. All of a sudden faces were tragic, and people were walking around in the hallways of our building and in the streets with inquiring eyes, saying, "Has it happened to you?" It was awful. It was like a domino effect: Everything that happened to one person gradually happened to other people who were connected with them, until everything just shut down. The people who had given my father the contract lost all their money, and since my father had borrowed all of that money, he was wiped out. Psychologically, he never recovered.

People jumped off the George Washington Bridge. We heard about it. People we knew who were involved with Wall Street couldn't meet their debts. They were so disgraced that they killed themselves in order to get their families the insurance money. It was incredible and horrible what happened in those years. Respectable businesspeople would walk around in the streets of downtown Manhattan with a tray of bright red apples, and they would ask you to buy an apple for five cents. And horrible as that was, it was even more horrible that we didn't even have five cents!

For about five years I had been saving money in a piggy bank. If I even had a penny or two, I would put it in the piggy bank, and I loved to shake it and feel the weight. One day I came home and grabbed hold of my piggy bank, just to give it a shake, and discovered that there was nothing in it. The bank was empty!

My mother was standing in the doorway, looking at me, and she said, "Your father borrowed the money. He has to go out to look for work and he needed the money to go downtown. When your father comes home don't say anything. It's bad for him." And he came home and I didn't say anything but my face was swollen with tears. And my father took me in his arms and he said, "I'm sorry. I had to have money. But it's a loan. I'll pay it back to you." He never did. But it was so embarrassing for me and so painful, even then in my childish years, to have to see my father in this terrible state. That's what was bad. My father walked the streets every day and found something to do. My mother went to work, and I even worked. My mother would find a few pennies and we would go to the greengrocer and wait until he threw out the stuff that was beginning to rot. We would pick out the best rotted potato and greens and carrots that were already soft. Then we would go to the butcher and beg a marrow bone. And then with the few pennies we would buy a box of barley, and we'd have soup to last us for three or four days.

Then one day I came home from school and saw furniture on the sidewalk that looked familiar. We had been evicted. What hurt me most about it was the look of pain on my mother's and father's face. I couldn't bear to look at them.

When the Depression began, most people in positions of power thought that the government should not tamper with the economy. They viewed the economy as though it were the weather: When it's bad, there's not much you can do but wait until it's good again. But the Great Depression wasn't just bad weather, it was a hurricane.

People had expected that the good times of the 1920s would go on forever. They never dreamed that the economy could collapse so completely. While President Herbert Hoover promoted the idea that the crisis would be over soon, ordinary people watched bizarre things happen. Unemployed lumberjacks set fires so that they could earn a few dollars as firefighters, putting out the same fires they had started. Farmers who could not get a fair price for their crops let fruit and vegetables rot in their fields, even as millions of people went hungry. In the spring of 1931 the people of Cameroon, a country in West Africa, sent New York City a check for $3.77 to help the "starving." American harbors were filled with ships carrying immigrants back home to Europe, where they hoped things would be better.

With factories and farms closing all over the country and no jobs to be found, some Americans left home and, in search of a solution to their troubles, began to drift across the landscape. People crammed their belongings into rusting Fords or Chevrolets or hopped freight trains to find work, to find a meal, to find a decent way to keep their lives together.

Bill Bailey, who was born in the 1910s, was one of those whose life became a scene of desperation.

I hit the road to look for work, but as the Depression got deeper, things just got worse and worse. And while people may have wanted to help you, with a loaf of bread or a sandwich or something like that, they had to start getting selective: Should they give it to a thirty-five-year-old man or to a woman with two kids? So bit by bit you began to see yourself getting less taken care of. There was this horrible law across the whole United States, called the vagrancy law. Any cop could come up to you and say, "Hey, you got a job?" "No." "Where do you live?" "Oh, I'm from another state." "You got any money with you?" "No." And then they'd have you for vagrancy. So I just minded my own business and tried to avoid all that by moving on.

Soon I discovered that the best way to travel was by railroad boxcars. Of course, the railroad companies were opposed to the idea originally. But in towns where things were really bad, the people were going to the sheriff and saying, "You've got to do something about all of these people bumming on the streets." Then the sheriffs would call up the railroads and say, "We want your train to slow down in this little town every now and then to pick up all these hoboes." So because of the pressure from the sheriffs, these trains would slow down and we'd jump on and ride. It wasn't so bad. Some days if the weather was nice, you could sit up on the roof of the cars and sun yourself.

Heading westward into California, we joined masses of people, because everyone was under the illusion that there was work out there. But who needed a hundred guys picking oranges anymore when there was no market for the oranges? It was a very sad type of deal. But I will say this: As bad as things were, there was no violence. You'd never hear of a woman being attacked or beaten. And all the mothers on the road with families, they got the preference in the box-cars. When you were making a grab for a freight car and you were just getting ready to jump in, somebody might be there at the door and say, "Sorry, fella, family car." That meant there was a whole family in there, and you respected that and you stayed out. That's just the way it was. As things got worse there were more and more families out there. Sad, but that's the way the country was.

So you'd just have to learn to survive—somehow. I'd go to the undertaker and say, "Anybody leave a good coat here?" Because often they'd take the clothes off the dead people and bury them in their Sunday suits. And the undertakers were pretty good guys, so they'd say, "Well, why not? He don't need it anymore. Good luck." And if that stiff lying there was your size, then you were in luck.

Bumming was easy for me, because I was young and had a schoolboy face and I'd always say "madam" or "mister," and "I'm willing to work if you will give me a meal."

I've been in places where I was bumming at the front door and while I was trying to get their attention, I could hear a knock on the back door—someone else looking for a handout. Some people even put up signs saying, "Please do not knock. We have nothing for ourselves." And you always had to be careful that you weren't thrown in jail for asking for food.

Most of all, during the early years of the Great Depression, people looked for a leader, someone to point the way out of this crisis. America's wish for a savior would be answered by an energetic aristocrat from New York.

It's hard to imagine the hope and expectation that greeted Franklin Delano Roosevelt when he became the thirty-second president of the United States in 1933. He was the wealthy governor of New York and a distant cousin of Teddy Roosevelt. His legs were so crippled by polio that he couldn't even stand without awkward leg braces. But the task ahead of him was the greatest challenge for any president since Lincoln. Within days of his inauguration, half a million people had written letters to the White House to wish him well.

"The only thing we have to fear is fear itself," Roosevelt claimed. And with the help of radio, which allowed him to talk directly to Americans in their own homes, the new president led the country into a series of drastic reforms. In his first hundred days in office, the government passed new laws to help farmers, set up a federal relief program, establish a minimum wage, regulate the stock market, insure bank accounts, and employ millions of people. These programs, and others that came later, became known as the New Deal. Roosevelt believed that the federal government had a right to play a more active role in managing the national economy. He also believed it had an obligation to actively help ordinary people.

For most Americans, Roosevelt was exactly the leader they needed. In what were desperate times, FDR offered hope and inspiration. With his legendary "fireside chats," as he called his radio talks, President Roosevelt asked the country to give his plans for economic recovery a chance to work.

Marty Glickman, born in 1917, described the effect Roosevelt had on people when he became president.

When Roosevelt came to power in 1933, there was an almost immediate change in attitude. By that time Herbert Hoover was the losing president. He rarely smiled. When Roosevelt came to power, that voice . . . that brilliant, ringing, uplifting voice which we all heard on the radio made an almost immediate philosophical difference. We felt better about things. We felt we could win, we could get ahead, we could come out of the Depression. This feeling was certainly reflected in the activities of the adults around me. And I even felt it as a kid. I liked Roosevelt. I liked his smile. Herbert Hoover was a dour individual, but Roosevelt, with that smile and that lift in his voice, he was a leader, a true leader. Perhaps the greatest leader we ever had.

Actor Ossie Davis, born in 1917, also felt the power of Roosevelt's voice on the radio.

In traditional black culture, the church minister is the divinely appointed storyteller. He gives meaning to existence. So for the black community of the 1930s, the use of the voice to affect us was nothing new. It was just that of all the voices that I heard and respected and loved, Roosevelt was the master. He could reach out and touch everybody and sort of bring us all together. He made us feel that all we needed to do to resolve our problems was to come together, work out a plan, and do it. And me, a little black boy down in Georgia, hearing that voice over the radio, I felt it. It wasn't that he told it to Daddy and then Daddy told me. He was talking to little Ossie sitting there listening to him. He engaged my support and my sympathy. It was very much one of the reasons why we Americans never gave in to despair. He was always there to spur the troops on: "Come on, fellas! One more time, and you're going to get it done! It's going to be wonderful." And you know, you felt better about yourself.

The same winter Roosevelt became president of the United States, a new figure came to power in Germany. Like Roosevelt, Adolf Hitler became a leader at a time of economic collapse. Along with America and most of Europe, Germany was also suffering from a depression, with unemployment as high as 25 percent. But Germany might have followed a different path if its people had been merely hungry. Unfortunately for the world, Hitler's enormous popularity was also a product of Germany's lingering desire for revenge.

Despite Germany's surrender in 1918, few Germans accepted that they had been defeated in World War I. Hitler had been a corporal in the army, and he believed that the peace treaty, which was meant to punish Germany, was a crime. He blamed the Jews and the Bolsheviks for the collapse of the German "fatherland." At first the Nazi movement was dominated by people from the fringes of society. After the complete breakdown of the economy in 1930, Hitler's message of anger and revenge found willing listeners among the broader public.

Hitler's speeches on the radio and at massive Nazi rallies struck a chord in German hearts. With his finely tuned oratorical skills, he could hold a crowd of half a million people spellbound. Many people now believe that it was the emotional appeal of the Nazi movement, more than its political ideas, that made it so popular. Germans, suffering from economic despair, heard Hitler pledge that their lives would improve and that those responsible for their pain would be punished. Hitler promised to restore German pride and claim for Germany what he felt was rightfully its own: more land.

While Germany was cheering, Hitler ordered the arms industry to go into full production. If he intended to expand Germany's borders to the east, he would need to lead a powerful nation. Hitler also began to "punish" those he felt were responsible for Germany's collapse. The group Hitler targeted from the start was the Jews. Within weeks of becoming chancellor of Germany, Hitler had barred Jews from public service. By the end of 1933 Jews were excluded from universities and from professional occupations.

Like Roosevelt, Hitler used the radio to speak directly to his nation. Margrit Fischer, born in 1918, shared the optimism that Germans felt when he came to power.

I was born in the last year of the First World War, and from earliest infancy I was aware of Germany's hatred for the Treaty of Versailles. I remember very clearly my mother's grief over her fallen brothers and cousins, and my family's very strong antiwar feelings. The early 1930s was a catastrophic time for Germany. In Bremen, where I grew up, there were lines in front of the employment offices, lines in front of the food distribution centers, longer and longer lines every day. There was a great sense of uneasiness everywhere. So when this odd Hitler came along with his slogans that captured the essence of what was in the hearts of the German nationalists, then it became clear, even to a child, that things would change very soon.

At that time he never spoke of war. He promised us that unemployment would end, and that Germany would once again take its place in the world as a state worthy of respect. And I think that was probably the key thing, for the Treaty of Versailles had cut to the root of Germany's self-respect, and a people cannot survive long without self-respect. So this man was not only admired but welcomed, longed for.

As a young woman, I pinned all of my hopes on this new personality—the hope that now everything would be entirely different and better. I still remember January 30, 1933 [the day that Hitler became chancellor], very clearly. It wasn't a revolution in the real sense of the word, but rather a relatively peaceful transition. Now, suddenly, there were brown-shirted troops who marched around and made a very orderly and cheerful impression. The sidewalks were lined with people, there were nice marching bands, and there was a festival-like atmosphere everywhere. There wasn't any jubilation yet, but there was expectation.

The jubilation came one or two years later, after unemployment had really been fought and the streets were clean. At that time there was still no mention of war, and no mention of persecuting Jews, either, at least not publicly.

We had no television then, only radio and newsreels, and of course everything we saw and heard was terribly slanted. Before every radio news announcement the government played a beautiful fanfare that struck you to the very core. When you heard the fanfare, you went running to the radio thinking, "What has happened now?" It was very cleverly done, and very exciting. Whenever Hitler's voice came on the air, you felt a kind of inner attentiveness. It was always something special to hear him speak.

We were never allowed to see anything that would tarnish Hitler or the image of his leadership. Of course, we didn't see everything as positive. We were certainly not thrilled about the characters who worked with Hitler, for example. But we couldn't publicly rebel against the state. That was the price we paid, and we said to ourselves, "Well, we are really well off, and we have climbed so far." Basically people were satisfied. The fact that we had to keep our mouths shut and to guard against being too critical, that we were not entirely free, that was the price that we paid for this positive feeling, this positive, upward movement of our nation.

For the human race to be punished by a Hitler in the twentieth century was bad enough. But he wasn't the only tyrant who darkened civilization in the middle of the century. In the Soviet Union, the ideals and hopes of the Russian revolution were crushed by the dictatorship of Joseph Stalin.

Stalin had inherited his position as leader of the Soviet Union from Lenin. After the bloody civil war that put the Bolsheviks in power (at the cost of fifteen million lives) and a famine in 1921 that caused the deaths of more Russians than had died in World War I, the Soviet Union's leaders faced a dilemma. The revolution had been a struggle for the rights of industrial workers. But more than 80 percent of the nation's people were peasants whose lives had nothing to do with industry.

Russian peasants had eagerly taken the farmland from the large estate owners during the 1917 revolution. But that was as far as their loyalty to the Communist Party went. When Stalin took charge, he pushed for collective farms. Instead of individuals owning farmland, the land would be owned communally by the state. Peasants would work the land on these collective farms, handing over their quotas of grain or milk or potatoes. In return, the Communist state would distribute these agricultural products "fairly" to all citizens. However, few peasants wanted to give their newly acquired land back to the state. They resisted violently.

Over the first few years of Stalin's regime, millions of farmers were forced into collectives. This created chaos for Soviet agriculture. Peasants who refused were deported to labor camps in Siberia or were shot. During this period more than fourteen million people either died of starvation or were executed. Whole villages were destroyed, and millions of children were orphaned, set loose to wander the countryside scavenging for food like lost animals. But the peasants found ways to rebel. People killed their own livestock and destroyed their farm machinery rather than give them to the Communists. In 1930 alone they slaughtered a quarter of the nation's cattle, sheep, and goats, and a third of the pigs, feasting on them in defiance of the government. But this form of rebellion had tragic consequences. With experienced farmers murdered or sent to labor camps, livestock nearly wiped out, and farmland left untilled, Russian agriculture slipped backward, becoming even less productive.

The part of the Soviet Union where collectivization was most difficult and where treatment of the peasants was harshest was the Ukraine. Stalin pushed the Ukrainian farmers to the limit and still insisted that they were hiding grain from the government. In fact, the Ukrainians were starving, forced to hand over so much of their harvest that they had nothing left for themselves.

Death began on a giant scale in 1933. Five million peasants starved to death even as Stalin demanded more grain. Dead bodies littered the countryside. Millions tried to flee, but they were refused train tickets or arrested if they tried to escape on foot.

Eugene Alexandrov, who was born in 1916, was a witness to the horror in the Ukrainian countryside.

During the famine, when I was a student at the Soviet School of Mines, the government decided to send out some students to help the collective farmers with the harvest—those who remained alive, that is. So in 1933 I was sent with a group of other students out to the Ukraine. By this time the famine had spread all over the territory. As we traveled into the area we noticed that there were no people left anywhere—they had all been deported or starved to death, all because of collectivization. Sometimes we would arrive at a place that our maps told us was supposed to be a village and there would be nothing there—just bricks and weeds.

When we arrived at Uman, the village where we would be working, we went to the family home in which we were supposed to stay and found only one girl there, of about thirteen years of age. Her wall was covered with photographs of nice-looking, healthy people. They were her grandparents, her parents, and her sisters; there were maybe twelve or fifteen of them altogether. We asked her, "Who are these people? Where are they?" She said, "They all died of starvation. I am the only one who's still alive, but I will die soon because I have already gone through the stage of being swollen." This meant that she was now in the dehydration stage and beyond medical help.

Living among the villagers, I learned what was going on with collective farming. The peasants had to give all of their grain to the government, but the government thought they were holding out and hiding the grain. Some of them did try to hide it under a roof or a floor, or they would dig a hole three meters deep and bury canvas bags full of grain. But then the Communists would come with long steel probes and wherever the ground was loose they would start digging. And when they took that grain away, the family was left without anything. If a family had a cow or pigs, they would slaughter them, too. In the villages you would never see a dog, or a cat, or a goose, or a chicken. Everything was consumed.

In Uman there was a small pond for fishing. And one day a group of men who were still strong enough were fishing there, and when they pulled in their nets they found a bundle of something. It was a human head, the head of a woman they knew, in fact, who had disappeared. When the authorities came to investigate, they traced it back to the woman's neighbor. He had killed her and was living on her flesh. He was shot, of course. I also saw two people arrested in a railway station near Kiev. They were a man and wife, peasants from some northern wooded area. When we asked the chief what was going on, he said, "They are cannibals. They are doomed to be executed by shooting." In fact, they were half insane, because when starvation starts, a person goes through various stages. The first one is a tremendous desire to eat something. Then the person gets almost insane. Then weakness appears. These people who were arrested were already in the stage of weakness. They were trembling, and not at all steady on their feet. Soon they would get swollen and desiccated, so they were doomed either way.

Through it all, Stalin insisted that everything in the countryside was fine. Newspapers and the radio never mentioned the mass death in the fields. According to the government, the harvests were doing very well. Of course, many people knew otherwise. But it was too dangerous to talk. In fact, the world would not learn the truth about what happened in the Ukraine until decades later.

Whatever idealism Soviet Communism had started with was trampled to dust. The Soviet Union was now an iron dictatorship. Like Hitler's Germany, it began to revolve around the dominating personality of one man. Europe was in the grip of tyrants, and these men were setting the stage for a confrontation that would pull the whole world into war once again.

INDEX